TALENT MAGNET

Talent magnet

Getting talented people to work for you

Mike Johnson

FINANCIAL TIMES
Prentice Hall

an imprint of Pearson Education

London • New York • San Francisco • Toronto • Sydney • Tokyo • Singapore • Hong Kong
Cape Town • Madrid • Paris • Milan • Munich • Amsterdam

PEARSON EDUCATION LIMITED

Head Office:
Edinburgh Gate
Harlow CM20 2JE
Tel: +44 (0)1279 623623
Fax: +44 (0)1279 431059

London Office:
128 Long Acre
London WC2E 9AN
Tel: +44 (0)20 7447 2000
Fax: +44 (0)20 7240 5771
Website: www.business-minds.com

First published in Great Britain in 2002
© Pearson Education Limited 2002

The right of Mike Johnson to be identified as Author of this Work
has been asserted by him in accordance with the Copyright, Designs
and Patents Act 1988.

ISBN 0 273 65488 8

British Library Cataloguing in Publication Data
A CIP catalogue record for this book can be obtained from the British
Library.

10 9 8 7 6 5 4 3 2 1

Typeset by Northern Phototypesetting Co. Ltd, Bolton
Printed and bound in Great Britain by Biddles Ltd,
Guildford & King's Lynn

The Publishers' policy is to use paper manufactured from sustainable forests.

About the author

 Mike Johnson is a consultant and author based in the UK and Managing Partner of Johnson & Jones, a corporate communications consultancy in Brussels and the UK, which he founded in 1982. In addition to his consulting activities he is the author of *Winning the People Wars*. He is a frequent speaker at business functions.

To the JJ's and CJ's

Contents

Introduction

One of the mistakes that those of us who write about business and management frequently make is that we forget that those who read our material rarely have the luxury of finding the time to look at how global economic and social changes are impacting on their industry or their specific job. Often we are so involved with the ideas, concepts and arguments that we fail to consider the views, needs and expectations of the Joe's, Jim's, Jill's and Jane's, who make up Mr and Ms average employee.

Well, this time, it's different. This book sets out to do two distinct things. First look at the issues that are causing massive change in our workplace and how we can turn these to our advantage; second, offer practical, workable suggestions for every manager – from the CEO to the most junior executive with newly acquired people responsibilities – on catching and keeping talent.

This is a book for every manager who has ever, or will ever, need to recruit staff – and fight to hold onto them. As more and more line managers find themselves actively involved in the recruitment process, this book is designed to give insights into how to hire and hold people. It is a guide – as the title implies – to the strategies required to make your organization (and your piece of the business) a magnet for talent, today and tomorrow.

Finally, I don't believe that business books need to be boring to convey a serious message. So, settle down in your seat and read on!

MIKE JOHNSON
Hampshire, UK

Comments and good ideas on being a magnet for talent to mikeajohnson@compuserve.com

1 Talent magnets: who needs them?

You know, I think you and I have some of the same people working for us.

NIKITA KHRUSCHEV TO CIA HEAD ALLEN DULLES

Some people work just hard enough not to get fired, and some companies pay people just enough so that they won't quit.

LOUIS BOONE

Talent in the real world

In the three months leading up to the writing of this book around two million people in major global corporations got right-sized, downsized, restructured, re-engineered, and any number of other corporate-speak "proactive reassessment" initiatives. In plain English, they were fired, let-go, given the pink slip.

As a consequence, in meetings with senior executives who should know better, I get asked, "why should we worry about being talent magnets, isn't there a recession headed our way that will take care of it all?"

On conference podiums in Europe and the USA I look out at a sea of 500 faces and realize that in at least 30 percent of the audience the light may be on, but there's no-one at home. They still don't understand that no amount of short-term downturn can compensate for what's happening in the marketplace. We are rapidly running out of people; people who can think; people who can do stuff, the kind of stuff we need to get done if our businesses are going to grow and remain profitable.

So, what's wrong?

My thought, having interviewed hundreds of chief executives and senior organizational executives, is that, "yes", they sort of know the issue is there, but they have the idea (wrong of course) that someone else is doing something about it; that it's someone else's responsibility: marketing, or sales, or finance? Yeah. They bring in the money. Their real-world view, "if we need people we call that recruiter we use, don't we?" "Hey, what are those human resource people for?" "What do you mean Joe, we keep losing people to the XYZ corporation, go out and buy some more."

My argument, the theme of this book, is that today we cannot leave the business of talent to others. Every manager, every employee has to take responsibility for attracting and keeping people. How we do that successfully – in the real world – is one of the great challenges for 21st century business. And the real world is the issue. The challenge is how can an organization, a business unit, a department, or even a team become a magnet for people? How can it be a place where people want to work and want to stay, when come a rough couple of months on the Stock Exchange you may have to show people the door? Can you do that and still look like a place people want to work.

My contention is that it can be achieved, but it is hard to do. And it is "work", and it needs to be recognized as work and a hell of a lot better rewarded than it is today. Unless chief executives understand that people are the key to prosperity and get this message on the strategic business agenda, little will happen. Unless we begin quickly to specifically plan for talent acquisition and retention (and have our managers geared up to do this and rewarded for it too) we are just not serious about the future.

Lip service, a few cloying lines spun by the communications department in the annual report just won't do. CEOs and other senior managers need to not only walk-the-talk they have to learn to love to live it. This is where the wheels of the corporate limo usually come off as senior managers get confronted on the first tight curve with a cold bucket of reality. Phrases, spoken with a tone of injured disbelief, like, "you mean we have to not just say it, but believe it, and do it, too?" are commonplace in the boardrooms of corporate America, Europe and Japan. After 30 years of doing it your way (and getting rich doing it), the views, experiences and expectations of a 50 year-old senior vice-president and a 23 year-old college graduate are as far apart as anything you can imagine. This manifests itself in the organization's inability to communicate with the people in the business without resorting to corporate spin-speak.

So, we have trite phrases popping up in annual reports, analyst and shareholder meetings like:

- "Human capital has replaced financial capital as the scarcest commodity in our business." This translates into plain English as, "we are really waking up to the idea that we may have some people issues we need to look at quite soon, even the finance department is becoming concerned at the size of the headhunters' invoices."

- "We are devoted to developing our human assets for the good of our customers and shareholders." For this read, "The CEO and the CFO have decided to deal with the people-issues by putting numbers on them. They cannot call them people they need a financial/numeric term: assets fits beautifully."

- "We are determined to be the employer of choice in our industry." This reads, "we lost so many human assets last year, that we have to get an injection of human capital into the business at any cost."

As Jean-Claude Larréché, Professor of Marketing at Europe's top business school, INSEAD in France, says, "the phrase 'people are the greatest asset of our organization,' is quickly becoming the third great lie of business, ranking alongside, 'your cheque's in the mail' and 'our computer is down'."

Recently, the corporate-speak meisters of the communications department have discovered another new phrase, work/life balance (WLB). While for some enlightened firms this is a serious program with a bottom-line result in mind (as happy, cared for employees boost their productivity), for many it has become office shorthand for, "hey we have a crèche for working mothers."

But any lingering look at the people issues that face our organizations, quickly shows that glossing over the surface with quick-fix remedies and shallow words buys you nothing but trouble. Sure you can't be the best company on the block every single day, with the whole world queued up at your door. But if you don't treat your employees – and those you might like to employ – honestly and fairly news will travel and you'll be left wondering why no-one calls, no-one snail-mails, no-one hits your internet recruit site.

All organizations have downturns, but being a talent magnet is about the long-term, not the short-term fix. The day you have to reverse the polarity on your talent magnet and let people go, how you do it, how you communicate it, how you help them, is what will keep you in the "desirable" category long after your reasons for doing it are forgotten.

To loop around to where we started, a key reason that you may want your business (or your part of the business) to be remembered is that of those two million people laid off, few are still searching for a job. Such is the global need for talent (almost any kind of talent) that if you don't care too much about where you move, there's a job waiting for you. Much as the media enjoyed the spectacle of the dot.com meltdown in the USA and Europe, the headlines had little to do with the (literally) on-the-street reality. As dot.com after dot.com expired, publicly hundreds and thousands of ex-employees – albeit a little poorer – were snapped up by eager recruiters. Strangely this, for the most part, went unfiled and unreported. Having written so much about those precocious 20-year-olds making a fistful of dollars, the media weren't into writing a happy ending for them. The fact that they rode off into the sunset in a stretch limo to work at the cutting techy edge of some born-again dinosaur corporation wasn't what readers needed to know.

Everyone loves a disaster, and the dot.com debacle was just that, on newspaper at least. In the year 2000, over 200,000 e-biz erks lost their jobs in the USA alone. The fact that 2.2 million jobs were added to the so-called New Economy hardly ruffled the pages of the *Wall Street Journal*. Everyone, it appeared, wanted to see these people get their comeuppance – the fact that it didn't really happen wasn't a good news story at all.

Worse was – supposedly – to come. The early months of 2001 brought the first doom-laden warnings of an economic meltdown. Working on the highly scientific theory that when America gets a cold the whole world sneezes, corporate chieftains began to hedge their bets, first in private, then in public. It is believed by many that you can forecast the entire world economy for about 18 months by spending 48 hours up a Swiss Alp at the Davos World Economic Summit. By all accounts it was the most boring in years. Few CEOs were making serious growth predications and, indeed, hard on the heels (or skis to be more accurate) of that event stock markets began to take a pounding.

Quickly, the grim corporate reaper was on overtime as venerable names, one-time high performing darlings of the stock markets, started to hint, predict and then announce profit warnings. As the *Washington Post* reported, "First came the falling stock prices. Then a dramatic slowdown in business profits and investment. And now come the lay-offs." They were all too right: 26,000 at DaimlerChrysler, 14,000 at Motorola, 15,000 at GM, 10,000 at Lucent, 7,000 at Sara Lee. The list was long: WordCom, J.C. Penney, AOL Time Warner, Ford, Gillette, Gateway, Chase Manhattan led in the USA, and Europe followed suit, spurred by analysts' demands to show they were "doing something positive." The terrorist attacks on the USA in September only added to the list of firms predicting major lay-offs. But although this brought bad news, it didn't do that much for those who were still vainly seeking people. Why?

- despite the size of the reductions most of them are spread out over months if not years. In many cases they are through natural attrition and/or early retirement;
- many workers in hard to find skill areas are re-defined as consultants or contract employees and just keep on working;

- there is a definite smoke and mirrors magic working here too. Industry watchers say that the mere fact of announcing a significant redundancy program is enough to hike your share price. Later, you just go back to the old ways. Hard-nosed, numbers-driven dinosaurs, of course, just go the whole hog as it offers, in many countries, all sorts of tax exemption provisions;
- on close scrutiny there was a pattern to the job losses: overstaffed hi-tech industries who had mid-level engineers (often those they had trained themselves) were the major victims.

Yet those thousands and thousands of people failed to make much of a dent in the jobless totals. As countries like Italy, Ireland and the UK announced the lowest unemployment figures in almost two decades, despite a raft of closures and corporate cuts, the *Washington Post* had this observation on the USA "In an economy of 135 million workers, where 275,000 Americans each week lose their jobs, even a couple of months of 150,000 layoffs will only add 0.2% to the unemployment rate." The *Post* added, "Even as some companies are laying-off workers, many others are desperately seeking employees to fill positions."

And that statement is the key. There may be shakeouts, and there may be more to come, but we are short of people and going to stay that way. This means that managing the talent you have (and the untalented too, by all accounts) is going to be a very real need: CEOs, heads of business units and team leaders, ignore this advice at your peril.

Up the job chain

To understand why we need to nurture our talent, and find better ways to attract new talent we need to look more closely at what's happening to the world of work.

The realization that we have run out of people to work for us starts at the bottom of the employment job chain. In most western economies today, emigration up the job ladder is well advanced.

In my small Hampshire town, when you follow the bus down the high street the back advertising poster is asking you to become a bus driver. Reason? it's a lousy job and no-one wants it and they are all emigrating to better paid employment with more perks and prospects. This is equally true for train drivers, truck drivers and construction workers.

Nurses are leaving the hospital service in droves (provoking a recruitment crisis in some countries). Where are they going? Swapping long, unsociable hours for a medical representatives job with fixed hours and a car to drive. One hospital in Amsterdam has more than 20 percent of its staff positions open; in the UK, they are importing nurses from the Philippines, prompting them, in turn, to go looking for replacements.

My favourite restaurant in London's Chinatown can't get waiters, they are now forced to employ back-packing Australians and New Zealanders. As the owner told me, "my son is in computers and my daughter is in television, they don't want to work in a restaurant." In Paris, restaurants and bistros are closing, not through lack of customers, but lack of people to work in them.

Everyone it seems has moved up the job chain: hourly workers are now part-time, part-time workers have full-time jobs. If you want to work you can. I have used this joke a lot, but today it is true: twenty years ago as a visitor in New York, I was told to always walk on the outside of the sidewalk, that way no-one could pounce on you from a doorway and mug you. Today, you still walk on the outside, but that's just in case someone grabs you and puts you to work!

So, to get the arguments over with quickly – otherwise you may as well give this book to someone else – here are a few of the reasons why we are not in an economic meltdown, but a skills meltdown. Put all this together and you have the case for why any organization needs to position itself to be a magnet for talent.

A shrinking talent pool

Simply, every organization on the planet has seen its possible talent pool – its choice – shrink hugely in the last five years. Problem is, too few of them are aware that this has already happened. There isn't time to do anything about it now in terms of heading off the problems that are confronting us, all we can do is act intelligently with what meager resources we have left.

There are several key reasons for this. The main ones, that should really concern anyone who wants to have and hold talented people, are:

- demographics;
- portable skills;
- changing social/lifestyle structures;
- global opportunity;
- new competition;
- a dearth of leaders.

Demographics

To say we are in trouble is to understate the situation somewhat. Basically, across the former "west", birth rates have been in decline for decades. This translates into a people crisis of undreamed of proportions. Three figures stand out that give a useful primer:

- In the USA 11,000 people a day turn 50;
- By 2020, 50% of Europe's population will be over 50;
- Japan's population will fall from 126 million today to less than 100 million in next fifty years.

The picture is clear. How do employers fill in the gaps that will be produced as the over-50s retire, cashing out stock options and picking up a little "part-time" job along the way? There are two answers to that. One, you open the doors to a large number of immigrants (UN estimate is 125 million required in western Europe by 2025 to sustain growth), which is politically and socially unacceptable to most Europeans. Two, you move your business where the labor is available, in the process killing economic growth in the west (see Chapter 9 for more details).

The Japanese statistic just compounds the problem. To sustain their growth they have no choice but to import talent to do the work. If they are offering interesting work and a new experience, many westerners would probably jump at the chance. Judging by the amount of sushi that gets consumed in Berlin, Birmingham and Boston it shouldn't be too hard a sell. But being serious, it means that your business will have less choice and as the years pass, that choice will diminish further.

Other big numbers leave us with less and less choice. China says it needs 1.5 million MBAs to complete its process of industrialization. Right now it has around 30,000 MBA students enrolled. So where does it get these industry leaders from? The west of course. The new cry on the campuses of America and Europe is "go east young MBA-person." Incidentally, it makes a useful comparison to realize that in the US today, there are roughly 300,000 MBA students enrolled. This gives you an idea of the size of the problem, but also possibly accounts for why the streets of Shanghai and Beijing are awash with fresh-faced westerners who aren't just there for the egg roll and noodles.

Portable skills

Anyone who can look back ten years, will remember the good old days when bankers were bankers, oilmen (they were all men) were oilmen, and plane, train or auto engineers seldom strayed beyond another industry rival. How times have changed! Today, many companies across borders and across industries chase the same people. While IT/IS experts may dominate the cross-industry trade it goes well beyond that. Marketers now move between banking and fast moving consumer goods, project managers leave aeroplane manufacturers for construction companies and oil firms. Highly portable skill sets are all around us (and employers encouraged a lot of that), so we can hardly be surprised when, at the first hint of an industry down-turn, the best and brightest bail out to a booming business sector.

To put it into context, consider this:

Question: What do Fedex, Amex and Manpower all have in common?

Answer: They all have around 50 percent of their people working on IT-related issues.

Fedex tracks shipments and gets paid electronically; Amex needs to bill you as quickly as it can from those transactions in all corners of the world, Manpower does the same every time a temp employee gets an assignment. The people who work for Fedex, Amex and Manpower – well 50 percent of them – could seamlessly swap jobs without missing a beat.

The interesting question is, if there is a war for talent, does Fedex think of Amex and Manpower as business rivals who can steal its most important "assets", or does it just consider the actions of UPS and DHL? If people are the key, then it isn't just a breakthrough product or service, a great marketing campaign or a brilliantly negotiated take-over that will win market share, it's who you can get on your side to make it happen. But how many companies do a competitive assessment using those criteria?

Changing social/lifestyle structures

The days when you left college, got a job, got married, had kids, retired and died have long gone for many of us. Distinct groups, with often contrary needs and expectations are beginning to make their voices heard (more of this later) and need to be treated in different ways. However, these changes, once again, impact on the choice we have. Many people – more than a lot of us realize – don't want to work in industry, period. Others, because they have a choice pick a job that suits them. Unless we are able to offer flexible work options that meet today's lifestyle needs of everyone from a newly minted MBA to a 50 year-old middle manager who wants to work part-time, we are going to seriously reduce our talent options. Equally, organizations that were revered as icons of industry in the past don't make the grade with today's first-time job-seeker. In the beginning it was tobacco and arms manufacturers, today it is oil, auto and transport companies who have their work cut out to attract talent, mostly because they are perceived as dull rather than anything sinister. The other development that is beginning to impact is that many more would-be employees are inheriting significant wealth and opting out of careers in business, because they don't need the money. My own experience of this is my neighbor's son, who inherited $2million from his grandmother's estate and, despite having a class A degree from a prestigious law school and starting salary offers of $100,000 plus, chose to work for a charitable foundation at $12,000 a year. We can expect many more like that as thirty-something Americans, Brits, Germans, French, Italians and Scandinavians inherit significant wealth and make new-style choices of what they will do with it. Putting it in the bank and turning up for work on Monday at nine seems to be less of an option these days. Again, putting the limits on the pool of talent we can draw on.

Global opportunity

More and more young graduates are finding profit and adventure by going to other countries to work. Today it is more likely to be half a world away than across a border. London to Tokyo or Hong Kong, New York to Moscow, Paris to Rio – all are viable options. Trouble is, most of these people don't come back. Add to that the need for general managers, project managers, IT managers, marketing, financial managers, mergers and acquisitions specialists and the increasing cross-border headhunting activity and quickly the game has changed. More and more Euro-commuters are clogging up airports on Mondays and Fridays (estimates say that more than 100,000 executives and specialists fall into the full-time or part-time Euro-commuter category). These people refuse to move home and family, but travel to work each week, returning at weekends. Again, they are depleting our choice in the local marketplace.

New competition

It isn't only portable skill sets and the rise of global jobs that is depleting the choice of every business. Another – again too often unrecognized – threat is beginning to make itself felt. Much of the economic success and industrial infrastructure of Europe, and the USA, is built on small and medium enterprises (SMEs). While we may not have suffered too much so far, many major players are in for a serious shock in the years to come. Reason? Well there are two:

- Many of these companies are not sophisticated in areas like IT, e-commerce, marketing, logistics and organizational development. My own estimate is that these SMEs will drain Europe's major companies of up to 250,000 expert employees; the talent backbone of a business. What they will do – are already doing – is to target the number two or three in a major firm and offer them: a lot of autonomy, stock ownership, a better or similar salary and an exciting opportunity with less bureaucracy. This is the chance to be the biggest fish in albeit a smaller pool, but many, faced with no promotion prospects in increasingly flat mega-monster firms see this as a rewarding way out.

- Equally, many chief executives of these firms (many are family-run) have no successor. In Germany alone over 80 percent of SMEs have no designated successor to the CEO. Rarely these days, do children want to take on the father's legacy so the job goes to an outsider. Again this trend is depleting the majors of talent (often top management potential talent) it can ill-afford to lose.

A dearth of leaders

Wander into any MBA classroom in Europe or the USA and ask the question, "How many of you want to be a manager?" and see how many hands shoot up. I'll bet not many. Today's b-school graduate has more important things on his mind than becoming a leader of men, or women. Asking this question on several occasions I have been disappointed to see that most new graduates want to go into a consulting firm or a finance house, where their numerical skills are rewarded and any people skills are buried, possibly forever. This is a serious worry for firms that need to fill future leadership roles. Peter Peschak, the European head of ExxonMobil Chemical says that organizations like his that recruit graduates and turn them into managers are particularly worried. To make him even more concerned, he should take a look at the average b-school curriculum these days – people management skills seems to be absent from the agenda. To add to this dilemma, there seems to be increasing evidence that fewer and fewer people want that top job in marketing, finance, engineering or R&D. In global firms, top jobs translate into too much travel, too many late nights and the inability to do the things you like (actually create something you were initially trained to do). As Professor John Hunt noted in the *Financial Times*, "It is no longer a shock to discover on a management development programme that 80 percent of people in their thirties have no talent for, or interest in, managing anything other than themselves."

That view is upheld by John Quelch, recruited to lead the London Business School, who believes that the proliferation of MBAs means that while the management population is better trained in hard analytical areas, these skills don't necessarily translate into the executive talent required by leading companies. He sees the problem as a clear indication that we have lots of numerate executives but few real leaders. But real leaders are getting turned off by the long hours culture and the sheer lack of time to get everything done.

More and more top jobs are about pushing through unwelcome mergers, fighting for budget and headcount and trade-offs with other departments. Smart managers – and especially smart specialists with few or zero people responsibilities – see this and decide there are other, saner ways to make a living inside a corporation.

All these forces impacting on every business make for a pretty nightmarish scenario. The worrisome thing is that a lot of organizations don't seem willing or able to confront all these various elements and see what – when put together – they mean. The likely outcome is that over the next five years, companies that don't look closely at these developments and trends will find themselves starved of the people they need to grow. Having said that, such is the need of organizations for new people that there is no way we can all hire the best people. Therefore, a lot of the talent we are going to have to manage is going to be, at best, average. I call it the art of managing mediocrity (of which more later). Mike Staunton, director of Motorola University in Europe agrees and says that, "the ability to get above average work out of average, or below average, employees will become a new core skill for managers." With the shift of people into new relationships with their employer, we will live in a new age where inability to hold people can create a huge downside.

Wooing the workforce

What we have already made clear in this introduction to some of the Talent Magnet issues is that we cannot go on treating people of different ages, experiences and expectations in the same way. Greeting an employee on their first day and giving them the employee manual and saying "read this" isn't quite enough. Surprisingly it is still standard practice in many businesses. What we have to accept – whether we like it or not – is that different people, from different age groups, geographies and educational backgrounds all have different needs. Failure to address that again limits our choices for the future, but also sends out a message that "we don't care."

While this is not a textbook, it is important for all managers and team leaders to get an idea of what is happening as the workplace fragments into different groups with different hopes, dreams and fears for the future. Essentially, what this requires is a matrix where you have expectations on one side and options on the other. However, what I have done is to break down these groups into six basic, age-related categories: hopefully categories that we can all recognize in our own company.

Each of these age groups attach importance and relevance to specifics that the others may not. Recognizing this goes a long way to being able to offer these individuals relevant, attractive and workable job opportunities. As we go through the book, we will come back to these six categories time and again. Remember, it is vital to understand that we need to be able to tailor a job to its expected output as much to the individual (or possibly the team) as we can.

The six categories I have used are:

- Twinkies (still at college and under 20);
- Point 'n Clickers (20–25);
- Generation X (25–35);
- Middle-aged and Manic (35–45);
- Growing old Frantically (45–55);
- Grey Tops (55 and over).

In setting out to be a talent magnet, each of these six groups needs wooing by the corporation – the anxious, sometimes clumsy, suitor. They all need different flowers and a different guitar solo to get their interest. The old-style company song, just isn't going to work. Our ability to choose the right flowers and play the right song – in tune – will be rewarded with their enthusiasm and commitment: at least for a month or so! Today's difference is that our repertoire needs to encompass everything from Beethoven to Puff Daddy.

Twinkies

This group is a tough call, especially for your average manager. But they are the future and somehow business has to appeal to them. However, they are light years, several galaxies and a few asteroids away from any senior manager. My old friend Hanneke Frese now a main board member at Zurich Financial Services once explained why she had left a very good job and a very good banking house as "I finally gave up on trying to bridge the gulf between a newly graduated student and a 50-year-old vice president with $10 million in the bank." She's right, the hopes and expectations of these two essentially alien groups is huge. However, we need them and we need to know what makes them want to come to work. Having said that, it's the wrong thing to say. What we need to know is how we can engage them to work for us. Possibly they will never come to work at all: this after all is the cyberculture.

Having said all that, do not despair, they are not all alien beings. There will always be a group that wants to do what others have done before them, be a CEO, make shit-loads of money, do the "power thing." All we have to do is find out which ones want to do what.

Point 'n Clickers

This is the group that we already think we know. We've read about them, but allow me to say that it is unlikely for all their collective wisdom that *Fortune*, *Business Week* and *The Wall Street Journal* really have their expectations of a career in business well mapped out. However, we are going to have to find people in this group to take our business forward, so we may as well do the best we can.

To do that, it may be useful to consider what both Twinkies and Point 'n Clickers on both sides of the Atlantic regard as their world. Recently, both the UK's *The Guardian* newspaper and Beloit College in Wisconsin, developed some thoughts that may help interviewers who can be 20 or 30 years older than the talent they are trying to hire. For someone born in 1982, consider these facts:

- They feel more danger from having sex and attending school than a nuclear war;
- They have never used Tippex and don't know how to use a typewriter;
- There have always been ATMs;
- Their lifetime has always included AIDS;
- They have always had cable and never seen a black and white TV;
- They have always been able to afford Calvin Klein;
- They never took a swim and thought about JAWS;
- There has only been one Pope;
- Somebody named George Bush has been on every presidential ticket, except one, since they were born;

- They were seven when the Berlin Wall came down, but are not sure why it was up in the first place;
- Michael Jackson has always been white.

This is a very Anglo-centric list. Look at it another way. Recently Portugal remembered the 25th anniversary of its revolution. With almost 50 percent of the population under 30, less than 25 percent of today's population were actually old enough to have any sort of significant pre-revolution recollections.

It would be good, wherever you are, to consider developing a similar kind of list before you embark on trying to recruit these age categories. Knowing what they know as their reality and what is ancient history helps – a lot. And don't think that this is confined to western culture either. In Japan there's a whole generation who are rejecting the "salaryman" lifestyle of their fathers. Growing up in an economic slump that has lasted for a decade, 20 year-olds have never known much else. Significantly they are rejecting traditional career paths like engineering and signing on as hairdressers and media-types. Many are happy just to live off their parents, prompting one observer to dub them "generation parasite." Still – like in Europe and the USA – they are the future heads of corporations: getting to know them might be a good idea.

But what do the Point 'n Clickers and the soon to follow Twinkies expect from a corporation? No-one seems quite sure. However, if there are two words that will define them they will most likely be "freedom" and "flexibility." These people, like the next category, Generation X, are not going to follow in the footsteps of their parents. They don't want policies, procedures, rules and regulations.

Recently at a conference I listened to the authors of the business bestseller *Funky Business*, Jonas Ridderstråle and Kjell Nordström, from the Stockholm School of Economics. They said one thing that every manager needs to take on board when he thinks about any of the new generations: "Remember," they said, "you are the best person in the world at one thing – being you." And that sums it up. The new generations want to "be themselves at work. And they will migrate to jobs that let them do that. What we need to do as team leaders, as managers, as CEOs is harness that enthusiasm for wanting to be themselves and do useful, meaningful work. If we can find the key to that enthusiasm and need then we have found a way to manage the next generation and tomorrow's organization.

Oil services firm, Schlumberger has tried to do this with an initiative called "Work 2020": getting employees to give their vision of their workplace and how it will be two decades hence.

So the advice is get flexible, and get with it. Don't try to fight it. If people want to work three days a week find a way to let them. If they want sabbaticals, help them do that. If they don't want to come to work at all use already available technology to make that work too. It is interesting to consider that technology has arrived just in time to help us, lap-tops, e-mail, intranets, mobile phones, all make us not only mobile, but able to work from a distance, even if that is our back bedroom. We are going to have to invest a whole lot more in that and we are going to have to develop managers that feel comfortable with a very diverse, demanding but ultimately effective workforce. All the while, of course, there will be a major group of old-style managers who walk around with fingers crossed hoping that one day these people will begin to assume "normal" traits. Well it might just happen, but don't hold your breath.

Generation X

Having said it might never happen, there is mounting evidence that Generation X has already sold out (partly) to the corporate dream. The issue here is that Generation X isn't weird anymore, in many corporations it IS the bulk of the employees. It is over 10 years since Generation X – a group, allegedly, disaffected with the way their fathers and mothers had worked, only to be downsized after years of loyal service – made it clear that they wouldn't make the mistakes of their parents.

So what did they do? They moved jobs a lot, they quit fast if they didn't like the coffee in the company canteen, they moved into hip jobs in new media and technology. Observers said they didn't like money too much, they worked because they liked where they were and their colleagues were all of the same mind. The word "phooey" comes to my mind. Why? Generation X grew up. Sure it marries later, has children later, but it still does what its parents did. It worries over mortgages and school fees and eventually it settles down to a steady job. Certainly, today Generation X is a shadow of its former revolutionary self. It is out there enthusiastically making money, grabbing power, getting on the career curve. More than that it is now at the top end (the 35 year-olds) getting into senior management. And while it may have some different views from older generations, if a Generation X-er has chosen a business career, they have mellowed. The only good thing is that they have pioneered the revolution in the workplace that supports flexibility and freedom.

Middle-aged and Manic

For anyone over 35, the last seven or eight years have been pretty good. Prosperity has been at an all time high in the USA and in many European countries as well. So life's been a ball for this group. But there are concerns – big concerns – on the horizon. They have done a great deal better than their parents generation, with all the trappings that even a moderately successful career can bring: large houses, cars, two or three vacations a year, private schools for the children. Their concern is holding on to this at all costs. In doing so they throw up a huge challenge to businesses everywhere. These are the people that don't want – at any price – the change that the rapidly ageing Generation X-ers and the Twinkies are going to bring. These are the sons and daughters – two decades on – of the middle managers that were disparagingly referred to by management guru John Humble as "the concrete middle." They were immovable, closed to new ideas, opposed to innovation. Now their children – currently occupying that danger zone of 35 to 45 – are becoming the champions of the status quo: a status quo that they created. Change, even though it is all around them is something to be sniffed at with suspicion. And as time goes on and warning signs appear in the form of falling stock prices, industry lay-offs and the like their fear is growing into a survival mania mode that needs to be addressed.

Interestingly enough, our Middle-aged and Manic group are the ones that suck up the management development budgets as we try (often in vain) to get them to join in the party. This is particularly true after mergers or acquisitions, where companies are desperate to build some new ersatz culture that all can embrace (they rarely do, so you can keep your dollars and euros firmly in your pocket). Of course, there are others who have forged new ways of thinking about the business, but the majority are spending a lot of time looking after themselves. They are also the most vulnerable to the siren song of the head-hunter, as their concerns for personal security, but also a better job, make them relatively easy pickings: a number two or three in the marketing division, can easily be coerced into going for that top job in a rival firm. This is especially true when sign-on bonuses and golden parachutes make it an easy – "no brainer" – type of choice.

Growing old Frantically

Above our Middle-aged and Manic group comes another distinct category in the upper forties and early fifties. Surprisingly, at first glance, this group is less worried on the whole than the group below. But a quick glance at the situation shows us why. This is the group that had its feet held to the fire in the mass downsizing of the early nineties. So it has been there and these are the survivors. Also if you looked back in time to the last group to occupy this sector you would also have seen if not complacency then a certain smug satisfaction. There are several reasons for this. Here are just a few:

- they are practically fireproof whatever happens. If it comes to involuntary retirement they will get well compensated and have – in most cases – well funded pensions to support them;

- practically all of them have a spouse that works too;

- In most cases the children are through college, so they have reduced outgoings;

- they usually own their house and have a little money set aside.

These are the people who volunteer to go, when the first offer comes along. These are the people who are well enough into their profession they can get consulting assignments or two or three day a week "hobby" jobs that "give them something to do." These are the people who take their life-time earnings and go live in Florida or Southern Spain. These are the people who wise corporations blasted out of their executive chairs in the last round of downsizing and destroyed all the knowledge and tradition in the company. Will they do it again? You bet, only this time these people are ready for the corporate axe-man.

Grey Tops

The first reaction when you talk about those over 55 is "are there any left?" The answer is: "yes, a lot." Having got it wrong once before with massive, so-called, re-engineering companies seem to have become reluctant to dismiss these venerable beasts out of hand. Belatedly they have realized that these people not only actually know something, but know the business inside out. Possibly far more important, they have also managed to take on board that these people know the customers so they are worth money to the firm. However, there is always a downside and this one is simple: many over 55s don't see themselves on the daily commute anymore. They have economic security (like the Growing Old Frantically group, only more so) and they are beginning to demand and get much more flexible deals about how, where and when they work. They negotiate part-time deals, become advisors, consultants, or external board members. They know full well they have a valuable contribution to make and they are adept at getting what they want on their own terms.

There's a rather ironic situation here. We seem to have come full circle. Our Grey Tops are demanding and getting a working deal that is based on flexibility and freedom. The same flexibility and freedom that our Twinkies and Point 'n Clickers expect from any employer. For those that have been predicting a new world of work for a long time, perhaps this is what it is, a working world where we all have our own private portfolio of tasks to be accomplished and we meet them in any way we choose as long as we deliver.

Turning full circle

If we want to be seen as a talent magnet we are going to have to build the ability to be naturally flexible into our operational culture. Today in most firms, flexibility only comes when employees threaten to quit or have a major lifestyle change imposed upon them. While a case-by-case approach may be OK in the short term it doesn't last for long. At the very least it breeds inequality and employee jealousy, at worst corporate chaos.

The sad truth about being flexible and offering freedom in any business is that it cannot be flexible and free at all, it needs polices and procedures to avoid anarchy. While I will deal with this in detail in later chapters, it is useful to look at some of the key trends that are shaping what employees expect of the business they work with.

The niche workplace

A decade after niche marketing burst into our work lives (well it did in the marketing departments of some companies!) the drilling down to find smaller and smaller segments to focus on has come to the job itself. People are already seeking out workplaces and individual jobs that match their values, expectations, personality and lifestyle. Today, there is a broader range than ever to choose from. If you are a high-tech cool customer, you'll go for a start-up (yes, even in rough times) where you can play video games in your downtime. If you are creative, you'll head for a new media organization in New York or London's Soho. If you are the caring kind, you'll go to a global charity or not-for-profit organization. Organizations are already turning on that talent magnet by differentiating themselves from others – letting people know what they stand for, what their values are.

Watch out for employer of choice battles

This horrible phrase (already clogging up the chairman's statement in far too many annual reports) is set to get top billing in the business lexicons.

As I pointed out earlier, wanting to be an employer of choice usually means you have a problem and need to fix it – FAST. Those that are employers of choice – unless they are incredibly smug – don't talk about it, they just do it. However, real-life employers of choice (wherever in the world they are) have several things in common that we would do well to heed:

- a recognized and organized work life balance program that meets needs across the business;

- professional and personal development opportunities for all;

- the ability to make a contribution to the firm tied to personal responsibility;

- a friendly and culturally rich environment ("being with others I can relate to");

- a business that is responsible to the community as a whole.

The "I'm best at being me" syndrome

We all might want personal responsibility and the chance to make a contribution, but increasingly employees at all levels want to be themselves. The *Funky Business* author's "I am the best at being me" will manifest itself increasingly as employees demand that their workplace recognizes their needs and expectations. Studies on both sides of the Atlantic suggest that employees at all levels (from senior managers to office juniors) increasingly list the need for "personal authenticity" among their key criteria for job satisfaction. It is no longer enough to meet the needs for a challenge or a good salary, but to allow people to "be themselves at work."

Walk-the-talk or we walk out

The changing profile, demands and expectations of employees, coupled to an increasing shortage of talent, will put huge pressures on managers. Knowing they have control, employees will take an increasingly activist stance and will demand and get their worth recognized. And this will happen across the board from a newly-minted MBA to a 50 year-old middle manager who wants to work part-time. If we don't recognize these undercurrents already stirring in our firms we are going to seriously reduce our talent choices.

Let's be ethical too

In the beginning it was tobacco and arms manufacturers, today it is oil, auto and transport companies who have their work cut out to attract a whole group in society who don't see their way of doing business as something they want to get involved in. Again, this reduces the choices of some companies still further.

A new renaissance?

Work will be just a part of what we do and who we are. It will become a cycle of work, further education, personal pursuits. Neither will there be any official finish line based on age. Some people will "retire" early while others will work on for either fun or financial reasons.

Management expert Tony Buzan suggests that we are, in fact, entering a new renaissance, and it "would be a good idea for governments to begin to recognize this." He believes that, "virtually all utopian visions have been totally the opposite of the way we live today: no-one worked, everyone played. Like the Greek and Italian Renaissance they are devoted to the mind, to physical things, to art and sport." Buzan reckons that we are entering a new age ("Just look at all those magazines about leisure"). When you consider that there are millions of millionaires in Europe and the USA, what will they do for "work": sail around the world, grow prize-winning roses, become a patron for some struggling artist or sports-person, work for a charity? "We can support this 'career' pattern," says Buzan, "because an increasingly large number of people don't need to work in the old sense of the word."

Now how would this pattern of work, education and personal pursuits play with the average corporation? But if we want to capture talent and more importantly get it to turn up on our doorstep we need to consider these ideas which are no longer "out-of-the-box" but very much a growing day-to-day reality.

While it doesn't go quite as far as to embrace this renaissance theory, a new law in the Netherlands captures the mood. It is now legal for an employee to request to only work four days a week (for one day's less salary), and this must be honored and the job guaranteed by the employer. This is certainly a trend in Europe (think France's 35-hour-a-week experiment). Indeed college students in a survey of five European countries said they didn't want to work longer than four days a week (three would be ideal) and had plans to build a career on that basis. Other studies in the USA and the UK show a marked increase in employees who would trade salary for more time off. In Belgium, go-ahead firms like mobile phone company Orange already do that (you can exchange bonus cash for days) and a large number of employees take up the option. Top management would do well to heed this trend and consider what failure to do so does to their attractiveness as a talent magnet.

There are – it has to be said – companies that "get this" new wave of need. Sara Lee's operations in Australia have a work contract that actually says, "there are no fixed hours." We don't care when people come to work as long as they achieve what we agree their work responsibilities are," says Ian Cormack a senior HR executive. In the UK, Dutton Engineering has introduced a working year. Employees work a fixed number of hours per year, with the plan that they increase their presence when things get really busy. In Belgium, the printing firm Casterman have a workweek that lasts only a weekend – Friday night to Sunday night plus one full Friday every fortnight. There's a queue to volunteer.

Start thinking of maximizing minorities

We are still not using the minorities in our societies very well.

Immigrants

While the USA tries ever harder, most of Europe stumbles. Countries like France, Germany, Belgium and Holland all have large immigrant minorities (Turks, Algerians, Moroccans and so forth) who are not making it, even after three generations into mainstream business. Many of them become increasingly angry at being disenfranchised, as few ever break through the glass ceiling that prevents their integration. Others who start their own businesses find it hard to do business with mainstream corporations. As we will see later (Chapter 9) failure to begin to integrate this group of talent is storing up not-so-long-term trouble. Not only that, without encouraging this group, many countries will find themselves unable to not only increase their growth, but even have the ability to sustain it. If you as a business cannot contemplate the idea of a major change in the racial and religious mix of your workforce, you will have a problem – it's called being starved of talent. As Göran Lindhal, then president and CEO of ABB explained in an interview, "in a few more years we will [need to] draw more and more talent from emerging markets. Talent, for example, that is rooted in Buddhist, Muslim and Hindu cultures. How are we going to make that stick?" How indeed? Most organizations don't even know how to start that discussion. But they are going to have to do so. Without it you will not only starve at the bottom of the business, but you'll have no experts and no new managers either. Ah! Being a talent magnet isn't about being glitzy and perceived to be a great place to work… it's about knowing what is really happening out there in the real world and capitalizing on it in the best way you can.

The socially disadvantaged

Technology brings the ability for many long-term unemployed, out-of-work single mothers and the handicapped to do meaningful work that gets them away from welfare dependence. Companies need to think through this a whole lot more. Examples include enabling a single mother to be an "at home" call centre, fielding enquiries from customers in another time zone when her children are in bed. Simple, inexpensive technology makes these sort of options open to companies, creating a new talent pool.

Sandwiched employees

Our caring society has created a major problem that few are fully aware of – people live longer and longer and longer. Because of this, many employees find themselves with the double whammy of dealing with both child care and eldercare; sandwiching employees in a vice that creates stress and causes major money worries. Corporations have to recognize this (in some countries the figure for "sandwiched" employees in the workforce is put at 20 percent and rising) and have flexible systems that can help employees either cope or find alternative options. Failure to do this puts a lot of unhappy talent on the market that will gladly work for someone who can help to solve or alleviate these problems.

Women

In many countries and industries, women are still not recognized as key players in business and some wonder if they ever will be. The fallout from the major corporations (often due to frustration at the lack of recognition or opportunity) shows little sign of abating. Industries like oil and gas, engineering, transport, financial services are, in the main, still boys clubs. But if you want to be a talent magnet is it to be a "men only" magnet and can you afford that to happen? As the managing director of *The Guardian* newspaper in the UK, Carolyn McCall says, "the glass ceiling has not been shattered, which is contrary to what many men in business probably feel. I think a lot of men in business think the floodgates are well and truly open. However, there has been an enormous change and women are running businesses in many sectors of the economy: advertising, media, consultancy, search and selection, travel."

Well Carolyn, your sentiments are appreciated, but the reality is not what you say, in those industries listed above, no-one really cares that you and others haven't made it. Women are still being successful in jobs perceived – by men – to be easy, fluffy and fun. Having said that, some people are trying to change that. Heinz Fischer – an ex Hewlett Packard HR man (for 25 years), went to Deutsche Bank and set about a change process when he discovered that women managers accounted for less than 15 percent despite making up more than half the bank's workforce. The jury is still out on what progress he is making. And just in case we delude ourselves into thinking that the women in management initiative is going anywhere soon, let's remember that less than one percent of executive directors in the USA are female. But we are running out of options, and it may be time to change that – SOON! Although I think I first wrote that last sentence about 20 years ago!

Get ready for a rush of retirees

Again, too few senior executives have really thought through or even begun to admit just how much talent is on the brink of departure, which is strange, as in many cases it includes themselves! Some companies in the USA say that they are facing the loss of up to 60 percent of their executive talent pool over the next three to five years as the 55s and over take the money and run to the country club (not surprising when nearly half of the workforce in the USA is nearly 50 or over). The story is the same in Europe and Japan. The biggest concern here is that there are few replacements – the downsizing of the early '90s took care of that. So companies are going to have to turn on that talent magnet just to get these Grey Tops to stay – even for a few valuable hours each week. Savvy managers say that they are already putting highly flexible, and lucrative offers in place that include:

- part-time assignments;
- mentoring roles;
- telecommuting (cross state/cross-border);
- shared jobs;
- variable pay, based on time worked and goals met.

The situation varies from country to country, industry to industry, but in some it is a lot worse than others. The slow moving tide of seriously rich senior bankers in their mid-40s baling out of business threatens to become a flood, causing major problems as work is by no means slack in a world dominated by mergers and acquisitions and obsessed with market performance. These well-off individuals can start their own business, become day-traders or join a small less hectic firm. While rich 40-somethings may not be the norm in other industries it is true that many people made money in stock and they have already cashed out making them financially independent. Understanding what motivates these people to continue to show up for work might be a good idea – although the truth might be an eye-opener! However, the closed world of banking may be beginning to recognize that the writing is very much on the wall. "We need to do more as an industry to become more diverse in terms of ethnicity and gender," says Sandy Campbell, head of HR for global markets at UBS Warburg. This is good news, UBS Warburg won't have to look very far, there are a lot of women, immigrants and the currently disadvantaged just waiting to help out.

And what about that reputation thing?

As we will see in the coming chapters, reputation – or perhaps more accurate, perceived reputation – may certainly attract, and may then help to hold people. But don't be too sure. Life today is fast and furious. A bad rep today leads to a good rep tomorrow. Company A throws out 10,000 people and the analysts applaud and the would-be worker eventually beats a path to their door. Why? Because the stock looks good, opportunities look good (they are lean and mean) and they have swept away all the dead wood allowing people to, wait for it, "be themselves at work." The fact that this is the only way they can get people is irrelevant. Why? Because this is the new way of doing business.

And, something everyone needs to keep in their heads. Perhaps we can't keep people for very long. I don't mean for ever, or for 20 years (which we don't want to anyway), but even for a couple of years unless we learn to play the new game and learn the new rules (which get made up every time you play the game). Maybe what we should be considering is that our success, our ability to hire in talent, is based on one thing: that we can hire people faster and hold people longer than our competitors, because we do all these things that employees demand. Could that be the new success factor?

What we need to realize, and soon, is that corporate popularity is, at best, ephemeral. We write-off organizations only to see them rise again from the ashes. Conversely, we give huge strokes to businesses that never, ever, deserved it.

Here's an example. *Business Week* magazine, 29 November 1999. The headline reads *Outta Here At Microsoft, the software giant is losing key talent to the Internet.* The text explains that, "after 24 years as a talent magnet, Microsoft is grappling with a brain drain."

In similar vein the *International Herald Tribune* has a business section lead on 29 March 2000 that says, *Cisco Roars to No 1 as Microsoft Drifts.* And it says, "more than a third of Cisco's 29,000 employees have joined the company in the past year…"

Ah! What a difference 15 months make.

Microsoft comes charging back with new services, new products and a new focus that puts it back on the prime-time recruiters listing (some say it is even fun to work there again!). At the same time Cisco dives out of control shedding thousands of employees in its profits plunge.

Hey reader! Welcome to the real new world of the 21st century, where, unlike the '50s, '60s, '70s, '80s and '90s, you don't just get a good degree and go and work for Exxon, Shell, P&G, IBM, Siemens, Philips and the like, you choose what's hot on the market that month and plan to stay awhile – maybe.

The truth about your reputation is that it can be unmade in a couple of keystrokes in a Wall Street dealing room. Basically, we are looking at shorter times to be perceived as a great place to work.

What this means for all of us – is that:

- we will have shorter spans of being popular as businesses. The longer we can hang in the better though so we need to find better ways to manage that process and shorten the downtime between industry darling and industry dunce;

- going down faster, means we can come back quicker if we get the next business wave right;

- perception management will grow: managing the corporate reputation needs big bucks thrown at it and needs to change its message constantly to attract the right kind of people;

- don't look for long-stay talent, learn to manage a fluid workforce;

- that somewhat bizarre idea, employee branding, is consigned to where it should be – the garbage can. You can brand your business, your products, your service, but not your people. They belong to themselves, not you. Remember they want to be THEMSELVES at work. Advice: don't stick labels on talent, they don't really want it and they won't thank you for it. If they feel good about your business they'll let you know and they'll tell others on their own terms – not yours.

Are we trying hard enough?

The answer to that is "no". Few of us, team leaders, business unit chiefs and top managers in their cosy headquarter corner offices give enough thought to the concept of being a magnet for talent. They ought to. The signs are clear. But no-one is paying too much attention.

As part of the research for this book we asked M-World, the internet site of the American Management Association, to ask some critical questions (in early 2001) about organizing to be a talent magnet (you'll see other responses throughout the book). As a kick-off we asked two questions:

- Do you think your company does enough to be a magnet for new recruits?
- Are you personally trying to make your part of the business a place that people want to work and stay?

A couple of hundred people responded, none of them were CEOs they were just regular Joe's, Jim's, Jll's and Jane's. Here are their views:

Do you think your company does enough to be a magnet for new recruits?

Yes, sometimes	42%
Not really	42%
Yes, a great deal	16%

There's only one number that matters here, 16 percent. Basically the rest are irrelevant. Given the global evidence of a major ongoing people famine, that nothing short of total economic meltdown can defuse, if organizations don't burn to be a talent magnet no-one is going to help them and no-one will ever beat a path to their door. If you think you score alongside those 16 percent, go out and have a beer. If you don't for goodness sake keep reading! The scary part is that employees of big corporations think that little is being done.

Are you personally trying to make your part of the business a place that people want to work and stay?

Yes, all the time	62%
Yes, sometimes	31%
Not really	4%
Don't think that's my job	3%

Now here's a set of totally different responses by the same people. They, as individuals ARE trying to make a difference. Will someone please let top management know that. Oh, and for those top managers who ever get to read this, please note that all the responses were made on company time!

Who knows best?

Could it be that the employees – albeit intelligent, well informed employees for the most part – can see more of the upcoming troubles than senior management, who they don't think are doing anything like enough to get ready for the future? Yes, it very well could. In other surveys I have carried out, it often seems that top management have blinkers on, can only see what they want to see, or are so obsessed with a part of the business (more of that later too), there's no energy left for other concerns.

If 62 percent regard it as their job (these were in the main middle managers) to attract and retain people, but only 16 percent thinks their company is doing a good job of it, there is a serious gap between what the middle sees and what the top believes are the big issues.

Everyone needs talent, and we are going to need more than ever before. Without top management's commitment we won't be able to get the talent we need. Without their investment and energy in making the business a magnet, a beacon for talented individuals, there will be no company to concern us. The worry should be that the bright individuals, like those that answered our questions, will know that all is doomed to failure before anyone else and they will go where the magnetic pull is strong. As Obi-Wan-Kenobi said, "Let the force be with you."

Hey that could be a great new-age slogan for a cool place to work. And talking of cool places to work let's move on to Chapter 2 and look at what that means in terms of reputation and perception.

NINE VIEWS OF BEING A TALENT MAGNET

These views are insightful. They are a very mixed bag of people and professions, but they provide a great insight into how those of us in business see the talent issue and how we can all do better at being a magnet for talent.

These aren't CEOs of Fortune 500 companies. These are people who listen to and speak with real people every day. They work with them, live with them, and most of them are concerned about them and their futures. At first I thought I would use these as an anonymous collation, picking out the bits that best showed their worries about creating their businesses as magnets for talent. But re-reading them made me realize that they are personal views and, as such, they deserve their own place in this book. Indeed the variety of the viewpoints shows that we have to consider carefully both who we want to work for us and how we would go about baiting the hook to get them. What we also have to consider carefully – especially if we work for a big corporation – is that the little guys are already celebrating flexibility and freedom as you will see in these comments. When it comes to being a talent magnet, these guys already know what to do.

DON BATES:
Managing Director, Media Distribution Services, New York City

Q   Does your company do enough to be a talent magnet for new recruits?

A   No.

Q   Are you personally trying to make your part of the business a place that people want to work in and stay?

A   Yes.

Q   Who do you think should be responsible for making the organization a magnet for talent?

A   Certainly top management, but when you really think about the proposition the answer is "everyone in the organization", since everyone has a stake in the business's future and everyone contributes to how it is perceived.

Q   For which company would you most like to work?

A   Microsoft.

Q   Why would you choose that firm as a talent magnet?

A   They create great products. They are very profitable. They value and reward intelligence. They provide satisfying jobs. They offer opportunities for getting wealthy.

Q   Which company would you least like to work for?

A   Any company that contributes little to human development. That exploits rather than creates. That imitates rather than innovates. That treats people as plug-ins for jobs.

Q   Why would you choose them as a turn-off for talent?

A   There is little or no room for creativity, innovation or satisfaction.

Q   What is your personal recipe for making your firm or your own department a magnet for people?

A   Give people meaningful work. Train them well. Treat them special. Pay them adequately. Provide them with opportunities to learn and advance.

Q   What is the thing that companies always seem to do wrong that turns off talent?

A   They don't challenge employees to contribute to the company's development, to see everyone as important – if not essential – to the company's success.

MIKE DEVLIN:
Director of Communications, the United Nations World Water Program Headquarters, Sri Lanka.

Q   Does your company do enough to be a talent magnet for new recruits?

A   No, but we're getting there.   ➜

Q   Are you personally trying to make your part of the business a place that people want to work in and stay?

A   Yes. This is the main thing we can offer our high potential people. Just as important as salary especially for young professionals. We offer them challenge, autonomy, responsibility and the possibility to propose projects that they would like to do. They can't get that anywhere else in the country.

Q   Who do you think should be responsible for making the organization a magnet for talent?

A   Ultimately the CEO, it's all a question of creating the right culture, but each manager and group head has to make it work, they are the ones trying to keep the best and to attract the best.

Q   For which company would you most like to work?

A   This organization.

Q   Why would you choose your own firm as a talent magnet?

A   I have *carte blanche* to get the job done plus a unique market customer context (science for development) to work in that exists nowhere else.

Q   Which company would you least like to work for?

A   Any large old-style company (European or American) with the Japanese as the very worst to work for.

Q   Why would you choose them as a turn-off for talent?

A   From what I can see these organizations value the process more than the people. It is a sterile, dehumanizing environment. They still place value on age and seniority and people have to do their time before they get responsibility.

Q   What is the thing that companies always seem to do wrong that turns off talent?

A   Too much emphasis on rules and procedures. In some companies there's still too much of the "we've always done it that way" view.

JACQUES BOUWENS:
Principal, Russell Reynolds, Amsterdam

Q   Does your company do enough to be a talent magnet for new recruits?

A   We are in the search business. This means we should apply the same, if not higher norms, than for our own clients. The problem is that, although our profession is well known, people have in general never considered moving into executive search as part of their career plan.

Q   Are you personally trying to make your part of the business a place that people want to work in and stay?

A   Absolutely. Rule number one is that I am personally involved in every single hire for this office. I guard the front door like a hawk. In case of doubt we do not hire. Creating a fun, pleasant atmosphere with top quality people brings a definite strategic advantage.

Q   Who do you think should be responsible for making the organization a magnet for talent?

A   Everyone should be involved.

Q   For which company would you most like to work?

A   If I would choose any company other than my own firm I would be making a big mistake hanging around here, wouldn't I? If theirs was a better place I would be talking to them.

Q   Why would you choose your own firm as a talent magnet?

A   This is a place with good values, good people and careful selection at the front door. A magnet that reinforces itself.

Q   Which company would you least like to work for?

A   Organizations are like living organisms, going through constantly changing environments. Only the ones that are fit and take care of themselves have the energy, talent and commitment to successfully adapt to these changes. In my role, I am privileged to see the   ➜

inside of a lot of companies. Let me assure you that they all have their problems (typically these start at the top!). The quality of leadership, however, determines whether they can solve them.

Q **Why would you choose them as a turn-off for talent?**

A When it gets bad, it is really bad. In fact, a turnaround may be more costly and more time consuming than just starting all over again. It's like a marriage. If you don't maintain it it starts to fall apart. Once that happens it is almost impossible to put back together again.

Q **What is your personal recipe for making your firm or your own department a magnet for people?**

A Always walk-the-talk. Treat everyone the way you would like to be treated. Watch who you hire.

Q **What is the thing that companies always seem to do wrong that turns off talent?**

A Not treating people with respect. Not living up to the principles you agreed.

PATRICK LYBAERT:
Independent organizational consultant, Brussels

Q **Does your company do enough to be a talent magnet for new recruits?**

A Hey, I run a one man show.

Q **Who do you think should be responsible for making the organization a magnet for talent?**

A Every employee. It should be part of a strong leadership excellence culture.

Q **For which company would you most like to work?**

A General Electric.

Q   **Why would you choose that firm as a talent magnet?**

A   Emphasis on learning. Combining emphasis on business results with empowerment and people orientation. The challenge of being big when it counts and being small when it matters.

Q   **Which company would you least like to work for?**

A   Any company with a command and control culture.

Q   **Why would you choose them as a turn-off for talent?**

A   Authority out of sync with accountability, bad leadership with values not respected.

Q   **What is your personal recipe for making your firm or your own department a magnet for people?**

A   Providing clear answers on:

- Who am I? Allowing whenever possible the freedom to be yourself and building on your strengths.
- Where am I going?
- How will I get there?
- What is expected of me?
- How am I doing?
- What support do I get (mentoring/coaching)?
- What recognition do I get?

Q   **What is the thing that companies always seem to do wrong that turns off talent?**

A   Not doing any of the above.

LYNDON EVANS:
Director of marketing, Manpower Inc, Brussels

Q   **Does your company do enough to be a talent magnet for new recruits?**

A   No.

Q **Are you personally trying to make your part of the business a place that people want to work in and stay?**

A Yes.

Q **Who do you think should be responsible for making the organization a magnet for talent?**

A Ultimately the CEO.

Q **For which company would you most like to work?**

A Volvo.

Q **Why would you choose that firm as a talent magnet?**

A Great product. Culture of change. Well organized. Respected brand. Reputed to manage people very well.

Q **Which company would you least like to work for?**

A Any large consumer goods company.

Q **Why would you choose them as a turn-off for talent?**

A Employees I have met give me the impression that the culture is not dynamic and the management doesn't seem to care too much about people.

Q **What is your personal recipe for making your firm or your own department a magnet for people?**

A Reward people properly. Recognize and reward achievements. Provide opportunities for growth, training and new experiences. Allow staff to have their own responsibility areas. Appraise properly. Show you care.

Q **What is the thing that companies always seem to do wrong that turns off talent?**

A The opposite of the above.

JOHN JEFFCOCK:
Founder and managing director, Winmark, London

Q   Does your company do enough to be a talent magnet for new recruits?

A   No, but we are getting better. We try and learn from others. I came across a company the other day who had a brochure dedicated to recruiting graduates written by recent graduates.

Q   Are you personally trying to make your part of the business a place that people want to work in and stay?

A   Yes. I would like to see people queuing up to work at Winmark. We don't have interviews any more, we have meetings. The last graduate we recruited had a MSc in IT strategy from Umist (Manchester University Business School) and she loved the fact we had a meeting not a formal interview. She turned down a big IT job to work with us on less pay because we can offer her more autonomy, respect her talents and treat her as an equal, not an employee.

Q   Who do you think should be responsible for making the organization a magnet for talent?

A   I think all HR directors should be replaced by sales and marketing people for their job is to sell the company to future employees.

Q   For which company would you most like to work?

A   Autonomy (a UK IT group that grew out of Cambridge University). Because they are ambitious, professional, respected, entrepreneurial and I guess fun to work with.

Q   Why would you choose that firm as a talent magnet?

A   See above. However, I think peer respect is very important these days. Hence the first question you ask when you meet someone is "what do you do?"

Q   Which company would you least like to work for?

A   Any government department.

Q Why would you choose them as a turn-off for talent?

A Boring, unimaginative, untalented people. No investment, no respect and no pressure. Or a cigarette manufacturer or an arms manufacturer.

Q What is your personal recipe for making your firm or your own department a magnet for people?

A Having meetings not interviews. Demonstrating ideas. Showing people they have input into corporate decisions. Having a "let's try it for three months and see how you like it", no pressure sell. We also sell how great the people they will be working with are.

Q What is the thing that companies always seem to do wrong that turns off talent?

A Talk down to them or say, "this is the way we do things around here." However, that slightly depends on the person, I suppose, as some people really do love mundane work.

SUSAN STUCKY:
Founder and principal, Strategic Practices Group, San Francisco

Q Does your company do enough to be a talent magnet for new recruits?

A No.

Q Are you personally trying to make your part of the business a place that people want to work in and stay?

A Yes.

Q Who do you think should be responsible for making the organization a magnet for talent?

A Everyone, all the time.

Q For which company would you most like to work?

A Stone Yamashita (a San Francisco consulting firm).

Q   Why would you choose that firm as a talent magnet?

A   A consulting firm with a similar philosophy to my own and really good clients. A "cool" place to work and smart people to work with.

Q   Which company would you least like to work for?

A   Accenture

Q   Why would you choose them as a turn-off for talent?

A   Boring, old, too cookie-cutter in approach.

Q   What is your personal recipe for making your firm or your own department a magnet for people?

A   Provide work that is significant and meaningful to them.

Q   What is the thing that companies always seem to do wrong that turns off talent?

A   Take too long to make decisions.

PASQUALE MAZZUCA:
Director, executive sourcing and development, Belgacom, Brussels

Q   Does your company do enough to be a talent magnet for new recruits?

A   No. But then no company ever does enough to be a talent magnet. We have started a number of key processes to make ourselves more attractive to top talent; everything from our advertising campaigns right up to the way potential candidates are greeted during their first meeting with us is now consistent.

Q   Are you personally trying to make your part of the business a place that people want to work in and stay?

A   Yes. I am passionate about making this company exceed customer expectation both externally and internally.   ➔

Q   Who do you think should be responsible for making the organization a magnet for talent?

A   The best person to start the process is the CEO. Perhaps he or she should be called "The chief talent magnet (CTM)." But at the end of the day everyone in the company needs to be a "talent ambassador."

Q   For which company would you most like to work?

A   This is a tough question! My ideal organization is one where there is a common vision and goal where all parties understand what needs to be done and just get on with the job.

Q   Why would you choose that type of firm as a talent magnet?

A   Visionary leadership is the key to making a firm an attractive proposition to a prospective employee. Remember when you start to attract talent it get's easier. It is a truism that talent attracts more talent.

Q   Which company would you least like to work for?

A   Any company driven by short-term goals that pays no attention whatsoever to the human side.

Q   What is your personal recipe for making your firm or your own department a magnet for people?

A   Making an organization a talent magnet doesn't happen overnight. There is no silver bullet of cook-book recipe you can turn to. You need the buy in and input from every level of the business to make it work.

Q   What is the thing that companies always seem to do wrong that turns off talent?

A   A lot of companies are still not aware of the importance of talent and talent management. They need to change that attitude.

SANDEEP SANDER:
Founder and chairman, Sanderman Inc, Copenhagen

Q   Does your company do enough to be a talent magnet for new recruits?

A   What has been done well so far can always be done better.

Q   Are you personally trying to make your part of the business a place that people want to work in and stay?

A   Yes. And it is something that needs to be done at all levels.

Q   Who do you think should be responsible for making the organization a magnet for talent?

A   Everyone in the organization should feel responsible for this and remember it wherever they are.

Q   For which company would you most like to work?

A   Hopefully everyone would answer the same as me – our company.

Q   Why would you choose your firm as a talent magnet?

A   It is fun to work here, we are ambitious, we give everyone a chance to make a contribution.

Q   Which company would you least like to work for?

A   Anything in the public sector.

Q   Why would you choose them as a turn-off for talent?

A   Limitation to career development, no opportunities to enforce change.

Q   What is your personal recipe for making your firm or your own department a magnet for people?

A   Making everyone feel that they count. Delegating responsibility even when it is a risk. Offering opportunities that give respect and offer support and personal development.   ➜

Q   What is the thing that companies always seem to do wrong that turns off talent?

A   Pretend to consider everyone's input and then do the opposite. Or, "we'll do it the old way, because that's the way things are done around here."

Different people, different countries, different views. But, not all that much really. There are some great ideas in the responses, but, distilled down, most of them are just a common sense way of dealing with the expectations and needs of the new-age employee.

2 For goodness sake, consider your reputation!

Reputation is what men and women think of us; character is what God and the angels know of us.

THOMAS PAINE

Confession may be good for the soul, but it's bad for the reputation.

THOMAS DEWAR

Conrad Hilton is famous for saying that the three most important things in the hotel business were, location, location, location. In today's world, we may like to borrow from that idea and say that the three things that every business needs is reputation, reputation, reputation.

When Noël Coward said, "my reputation's terrible which comforts me a lot," you can quickly tell that he was made to write songs and plays and not head up a Fortune 500 Corporation – or can you? Over the years, heads of major businesses have made huge errors of judgement, deliberately misinformed shareholders, customers and governments and fought and cheated their way to riches. Most of the great industrialists were little better than the robber barons who went before them. People worked for them for the prime reason that they had little alternative: if you wanted your pot roast on the table on a Sunday you had to sell your soul to the company store.

Today, we live in a vastly different world. Mainly because people have a choice about how they work, where they work and who they work for. As we saw in the last chapter, the end of the 1990s and the beginning of the 21st century have seen the rise of the niche job. People can – and do – take the time to not only seek out the job they want, but make sure that the organization they work for has values that match their own. And it would seem that there is little sign – especially for the best and brightest – that this trend will diminish in anything but a long-term, cavernously deep economic recession. So, reputation is vital: maintaining it over a long period more important still.

What does reputation affect?

Few companies seem able – these days – to maintain a strong reputation for very long. Market forces and the complexity of running a modern business empire (rather like governments) make it virtually impossible to sail on serenely. One day, sooner or later you'll wash up on some rocks, sometime, somewhere: only the foolish would doubt that. That's why more and more organizations are taking a long hard look at this aspect of their business and beginning to realize that – like everything else – it needs to be managed professionally. They are realizing that reputation affects a myriad of things with internal and external stakeholders:

- stock price
- loss/gain of talent
- financial relations
- customer relations
- supplier relations.

Alongside those concerns, smart companies have also discovered another truth about reputation. It is the *perception* of your reputation that counts – particularly in a firm's ability to hire and hold talent. So, if you want to become a talent magnet, worry first about what people think of you – even if they are wrong, it won't help your perceived reputation one little bit. And throwing money at it probably won't help much either.

Whatever Exxon (now ExxonMobil) does for the environment, it will always be remembered by a large group of the population as the company that got it badly wrong over the *Exxon Valdez* Alaskan oil spill. The company has even considered an ad campaign to publicize its environmental programs but fears that many people – including prospective hires – would write it off as propaganda. Indeed Exxon must wonder if these things will ever go away. In 2001 there was an anti-Esso campaign featuring President George W. Bush under the headline "Esso Ate My Brain".

Sneaker seller Nike will always be associated (in the wrong way) with Far Eastern human sweat-shops, highlighted in an ongoing campaign in Gary Trudeau's *Doonesbury* cartoon strip, no matter how much money they pour in to correct the perception.

We may eat a lot of their product, but McDonald's has alienated a huge portion of the population of several countries (France and India are just two) incensed by its relentless creation of new outlets. The perception is that the burgers are cooked but the capitalism is raw.

Banks like Goldman Sachs, UBS, Deutsche Bank and others are seen as making too much profit and paying their high performers too much money. A huge number of bright, energetic talent wouldn't be seen dead working for them.

Motorola, a star of the '90s, destroyed its credibility and its reputation in Scotland, with a badly mishandled closure of a main plant during the mobile-phone meltdown. From a talent magnet it turned into a national pariah almost overnight.

Few believe that Bridgestone tyres' Firestone division can ever again attract any customers, never mind new employees. Its much publicized dispute with Ford Motors has tagged it with a reputation that no-one – even Noël Coward – would cherish.

Even the hi-tech end is up for criticism that affects reputation and cools down the idea you are a hot magnet for talent. AT&T America Online has been dubbed "the worst thing about the Internet," with its software called "the disc from hell." Who's going to answer a want ad from these people?

Can it get worse than that? Oh yes. South West Trains in the UK (part of the privatized network) cancel trains because no-one will work for them. Drivers, guards and other staff have been known to change out of uniform before they go home for fear of being physically abused.

And arrogance can get you noticed too. Cisco Systems proudly boasted to anyone who would listen that they had the best recruitment system in the world. It targeted, "those who already had a job", but got their interest anyway. They could hire faster and with better retention than anyone in the industry. Then came the crash and they were suddenly jettisoning people like confetti at a wedding. They will take a time to rebuild their reputation come the time rehiring begins. Bruised employees have big mouths and they talk.

Of course, there is another side to all this. One thing is worse than having a reputation, and that is having no reputation at all. If no-one knows you, how can they beat a path to your door?

Food and apparel producer Sara Lee faced this dilemma in Europe. They had hundreds of high performing brands (indeed they were eighth in *Fortune*'s most profitable company list), but no-one had heard of the company. Their reputation as an employer was non-existent. As an organization that was in a head-to-head battle with Unilever and Procter & Gamble for talent they had to spice up their reputation, "But first we had to be perceived as somewhere people would want to work," they said. "When prospective employees discovered the amount of autonomy we gave people, our diversity programmes that promoted women and minorities and the range of brands, they were hooked."

Changes in ownership can also trigger changes in reputation. Mergers and acquisitions are all fraught with danger. It is often not what the reality is, but how people – especially on the outside – perceive the new alliance or takeover.

The poor taste joke in Detroit is: "How do you pronounce Daimler-Chrysler? Daimler, the Chrysler is silent. If you were a graduating American engineer, would you rush to work with them?

Colorful, fun employer Ben & Jerry's the hippie, counter-culture ice-cream maker sold out to food giant Unilever. Celebrated as a crazy employer for their motivational antics like "come to work as Elvis day" there's a wait-and-see what the multinational will do for an encore; few see quiffs and sideburns sprouting in the Dutch headquarters. Similarly, UK sandwich chain Pret à Manger – which revolutionized the office lunch by preparing fresh sandwiches at every location – sold a 25 percent stake in the business to McDonald's, seen by many as a totally different culture. What does that do to perception and reputation?

Organizations grow and they have to change. If they are to get bigger they need professional management. Often there is a time when people realize that what they joined a company for no longer exists. Hundreds left Apple when it ceased to be a fun start-up and brought in professional managers like Steve Jobs' replacement Jim Sculley. Microsoft (although now another type of talent magnet again we are told) lost many top managers because it had become institutionalized and lacked the "seat-of-the-pants" creative atmosphere. So perceived reputation, like the tide, ebbs and flows. But, in this complex world, where top talent and hot talent is at a premium, we need to begin to manage that perception. Not just to tell it like it really is, but to tell the world what we are, and what we want to become.

There is no use having a great reputation for the wrong thing. If we are to recruit and retain the right sort of people to meet our future goals, we need to make it clear in the marketplace we want to draw from that this is the type of talent we need.

A great case in point is German multinational Siemens. They realized that the perception of their business and the reality were two very distinct things. Those beating a path to their door were all too often electro-mechanical engineers, when their business was more and more information technology driven.

They set out with a very deliberate plan to change that. What they wanted was IT people beating a path to their door. How they did it was to redefine the message of what Siemens was all about and where it was going. As part of this they re-educated internal and external recruiters and made getting the right people with the right message a key part of their human resources objectives. As an organization operating all over the world – with something like 50,000 plus employees in North America alone – it was important to get this initiative right. They needed to be known as a company on the cutting-edge of technology. A company that would be an excellent workplace for new-age employees.

As part of that, they not only sought to update their image in the marketplace, but also took very good care of the initial induction process. They developed a system that checked out how new employees felt about the business and what else they need to make them happy on, what they called the "4x6 basis". What they did was to check on new hires after six hours, six days, six weeks and six months.

Interestingly enough, many employers will tell you that the first days are critical. No matter what your reputation is when an employee arrives on day one, it can quickly sour. In areas where there is a lot of job opportunity, employers say that up to 20 percent of new hires (below executive/management level) will come to work on a Monday but leave on a Friday afternoon never to be seen again.

Then again (and more about this later) the company can be viewed as excellent but local conditions can change all this. One example is in Brussels where three companies, 3M, ExxonMobil and Toyota (all perceived as good local employers) are losing staff because of local reality: you can't get out of the company car parks at night because of the traffic. While people would like to work there, they are finding that the inability or indifference of local government officials to try and help the problem is strangling these companies of much needed talent.

The message here is, it isn't enough to have a good reputation as an employer, it isn't enough to have the perception that you are the right kind of place to work. It has to be more than that, each location is different and needs to be managed that way. Any communications or HR specialist that assumes you can create some global set of rules about reputation management is just one thing – a fool. Strange then why so many try to do it that way.

Of course you can have some basic tenets about who you are as a business, that's what drives a lot of people to your door in the first place, but if you are going to develop the right sort of reputation on the ground you need to let people manage local issues in their own way.

Most enlightened firms are finally coming around to the realization that:

- you can have a global reputation that meets the needs of those financial analysts and investors, as well as the top level you want to recruit;

- you can also have a local, or national, reputation that can serve you well for what you require in a specific marketplace.

If this is worked on correctly, an adverse reputation in one market will never, ever, impact on another at least for the purposes of securing local talent.

Here, Motorola is a good case to consider. While no-one in Scotland (see above) may ever want to work for the organization again (and no Scot ever buy one of its mobile phones), a world away in China, the firm has a reputation second-to-none. An early investor in the People's Republic, it has been seen as an organization that is a real "employer of choice" for local workers: putting training and self-development at the forefront of its local recruitment proposition. In China, few will even be able to point to Scotland on a map, and as long as the company delivers on its promises, and it has so far, it will be seen as the place to work.

The same story would apply to Philip Morris. In much of the USA and Europe, graduates shun the company, believing that its cigarette manu-facturing division is an operation that flouts today's business code of con-duct and that it is a moral issue too far to manufacture products that are proven to kill people. But go to the Baltic state of Estonia and you'll find that Philip Morris is the top employer of choice. They offer – for the top Estonian university graduates – fast-track development, state-of-the-art training and the opportunity to work outside the country. In the eco-nomics class at Tallinn's University you won't hear any stories about big, bad multinationals being told over late night espressos. The fact that PM and other western MNCs are creating a huge local brain-drain is for others to have sleepless nights about.

What is clear, is that if you are a local manager in a country or a head of a business unit you can influence by your own actions whether or not you are a talent magnet in your area of responsibility (see Chapter 4).

Destroyed by a keystroke

As much as the upside is great, that hard-earned reputation can quickly collapse, torn to tatters by one or two unhappy campers on your team.

Below is the text of two e-mails received in the course of writing this book. While the urge to name-and-shame is great, the possibility of being sued is higher, so we will (sadly) hide behind the anonymous cloak of company X and company Z. What it illustrates is how fragile any reputation is. While the majority of us may have the view that a company is doing great – that, as shareholder for example, we are happy at what we are getting, deep down, others know a different story.

If you were looking for a job and on the shortlist of either of these companies, the question is, "would you still take the job if it was offered to you?" Both of them, would be perceived, on the market as hot shop talent magnets with a strong drawing force. If you want the real names, I have the complete e-mails and we can negotiate.

"Mike, you're asking about work-life policies – amusing! Company X are shedding 6,000 jobs and cutting back in many ways. X are a company that say they believe their employees are their greatest asset, but they are yet to prove that. The attraction is how the company markets itself, or rather its products; the retention part doesn't exist. Sure, talent development committees and talent acquisition managers exist but it's the 'old boy' network that gets jobs. This company is worse than most for networking, but when you work out who gets promoted you can see why."

And another ... "Mike, having spent 35 years at a major multinational I have been through several holy grails and sacred cows of management. Company Z, where a lot of my ex-colleagues are, is going through a big one now. I think it is called Six Sigma and it's SERIOUS: it would be fatal to smile when it is mentioned. Of course the stock is rapidly going down the toilet probably soon to be followed by the chairman!"

And, of course, these days there's nothing so open to the world's scrutiny as a confidential document. E-mail anyone and you may as well take a full page ad in the *Wall Street Journal*. Worse still for any employer is to get on one of those "best employers lists" so everyone knows how good you're supposed to be and then the skeletons don't just rattle, they come out of the closet and boogie!

Here's how Robin Nelson of the *New York Times* described two cases.

"What if your branding efforts land you a coveted berth on a popular magazine's 'best employers' list, only to set indignant employees screaming false advertising? That's what happened to Merill Lynch. After it made *Working Mother* magazine's best companies list in 2000 a group of female stockbrokers who had sued Merill Lynch for sex discrimination mounted a letter-writing campaign to have the company's name removed." It gets better, or worse, depending on your point of view. "The women," goes on Mr Nelson, "have hired light aeroplanes with banners to spread their message at sporting events and are sending a delegation to Merill Lynch's next shareholders meeting. A Merill Lynch spokesman said that while the company had not reached settlements with all the women, its managers "thought" they had corrected the workplace practices that had prompted the lawsuit."

There are two points to learn from this story:

- Hell hath no fury like a woman stockbroker scorned, or possibly sexually discriminated against;
- One word you never use is "thought", because no-one believes you: they perceive you are not trying hard enough.

Bet this set back reputations at Merill Lynch for a while.

Here's Mr Nelson of the *New York Times* again. "Verizon (in its pre-merger days Bell Atlantic and GTE Corporation) landed on *Working Mother's* list of 'best companies for working mothers', not long after employees had gone on strike over the company's decidedly family-unfriendly use of mandatory overtime and other issues. A Verizon spokes-woman said that the list's publication soon after the strike was an 'unfortunate coincidence,' but that Verizon 'thinks the magazine's selection methods are valid and will try for a spot on next year's list.'"

Boy, we bet working mothers are just lining up at the factory gates!

What's that smell? Oh, we're branding our employees

There are still organizations around that think employer brands are just the best buzz phrase ever. More than that there are a whole raft of consulting firms that will sell you stuff so you can turn your employees into branded people. This does not mean that they have to wear uniforms, have tattoos on their forearms or foreheads or any kind of corporate body piercing. What it does mean is an exercise in futility that, often, does more harm than good.

As we heard in the last chapter, people want to be "themselves at work." They already know that they are "the best person in the whole wide world at being one thing – ME." If you try and tell them that they are part of your brand they'll be off faster than the chicken in the Cerebos Salt advert.

Of course, not everyone agrees with this view. *Business Europe* a twice-monthly report of the Economist Intelligence Unit reports that, "European companies seeking to recruit and retain quality executives at all levels are learning to apply marketing techniques in their HR operations. Developing an employee brand is increasingly seen as a winning strategy for managing all aspects of employee relationships." According to their report, "the employer brand is about deciding what kind of employer a company needs to be." They add, "most recruitment remains a reactive distress purchase, that would not be acceptable in marketing, where there is a planned and coherent approach to the customer."

In a utopian environment that might work. In the real world things are different. People join companies for all sorts of different reasons. As I have already suggested, what works in one country or region won't work in another. A reputation that is high in one city is low in another. People will buy the perception of the reputation, but employee branding is suggesting that they are all happy to be clones. The last thing companies need these days is to stick labels on people – let them find their own labels and use them is nearer the mark of the new-age worker.

While the base concept may have some useful ideas in it, employer branding as a concept should be buried. We are trying to get organizations to treat people as individuals, be flexible, create freedom. Employer brands do the opposite – they lock people in. And they lock them in often to the wrong ideas and concepts for all the wrong reasons.

The man who says he invented the phrase "employer branding" is Simon Barrow, chairman of People in Business, a consulting firm in the UK. His view is that, in getting talent on board a business, "recruitment advertising does have a role in portraying the employment experience accurately, but advertising, public relations, brochures and videos are worse than useless unless the brand itself is in shape." Barrow suggests that good employer-brand management has less to do with the smoke and mirrors of advertising and other communication tools, and more to do with making hard choices about the kind of experience employees are offered and the way they are managed.

My view is that, today, employees know well in advance what they want and they are going to go in and negotiate it for themselves. A bland brand ain't no good, a company where flexibility and freedom are at the top of the pile and it isn't rammed down your throat is more likely to get their vote.

The trouble with employer branding is it suggests that we are all the same. That may have been great in the '60s and '70s when you could relate to being an IBMer or some other clone in a white shirt and sober tie. Today's employee seeks to be different.

OK, I grant you that it can work for a short period if you need to get people hired in a short space of time, but otherwise no. Interestingly enough, one company that proves that employer branding is a concept that should really have been rooted in the '60s but was never an option is Benelux mobile phone provider Orange.

The situation with Orange was that it had to launch into the market as Belgium's third mobile phone provider very quickly. The only way to do that was to get known fast. What they did was to focus on young, talented, tri-lingual singles (for the most part) who wanted an exciting lifestyle, but weren't afraid to work hard either. They kicked off their campaign in discotheques around Brussels and Antwerp offering free in-company massages, laundry pick-ups, at-home nanny's for sick kids, a call-in supermarket and "cool" cars: the kind young people love, that don't make them look like business people or sales reps. The whole campaign (backed up by a very in-your-face ad campaign) was a roaring success: after 18 months in existence Orange was voted in a newspaper poll as "Belgium's sexiest company."

Now comes the hard part. They don't necessarily want those same people anymore. The people who have put Orange on the map are drifting away. The cutting-edge is over, like start-ups before them (Apple, Microsoft spring to mind) the daily management process needs another type of talent. But that isn't what they are known for. They have a brand, it is the wrong one and it will take a lot to change it. As we saw earlier with Germany's Siemens, they were known for being excellent at something they no longer needed to hire for.

Employer branding? It might work for a short while but it can be costly to change when it ceases to fit what you want from employees. Equally, make too radical a change and you can frighten the ones you want to keep away too.

Hold the olive and take the flowers away

Of course there are firms that fall for this employer branding stuff and then manage to get headlines that would make Ghenghis Khan cringe. Serve them right? Yeah!

American Airlines was reputed to have saved $100,000 in one year by removing the olives from the first class salads. Now what does that say about a business for goodness sake? Would you work for a business that takes olives away from the customer? If they can do that what would they take away from the employees?

Goldman Sachs (well OK, the excuse is that they are bankers) removed the free bowls of fruit they dished out to employees. Some people will obviously stop at nothing when it comes to cost cutting. They claimed to have saved a whacking great $2.4 million a year (about the same as a middle level employee's year-end bonus).

And it's not just the Americans who are mean. Adidas-Salomon in Germany cut out the employee cookie ration… enough one would have thought to have downgraded the stock.

Go lasso me a steak

Of course there are companies that are getting it right – this week, or at least until the next recession bites – and they aren't skimping on the cookies either. SAS Institute, the world's biggest privately owned software company hasn't seen fit to cut out the frills just yet. Consistently in the top five of *Fortune's, 100 Best Companies to work for in America*, it allegedly spends around $60,000 a year on M&Ms to top up the candy jars on employees' desks. Better is to come. The company, once described by an awe-struck journalist as "the nearest thing to a worker's utopia", is located in Cary, North Carolina where employees can see today's lunch (in the form of prize-winning cattle) munching the lush grass in the parkland setting outside their windows. No wonder they have an employee turnover that is a fifth of the industry's average.

Actually there could be another reason their turnover is so low. Like the Hotel California in the song by the Eagles "You can check in any time you like but you can never leave." What do I mean? Well like Gateway, Microsoft and a few savvy others they aren't playing hard ball in the cut and thrust job market of Silicon Valley. Join SAS Institute and it's a long way to the next job interview. Similarly, Bill Gates isn't just good at computing, he can read the map and knows just how far Seattle is from anywhere else with a need for high-tech talent. The only competitor in Seattle is (or in the light of recent mega job cuts perhaps "was") Boeing and they make aircraft not software.

This is something that many of us could learn from. There are two ways of getting talent – you go where

- the talent is huddled together (e.g. Silicon Valley) and you go out and recruit;
- there is no talent at all and import it.

Both have upsides and downsides and depend on what kind of perception you can create with prospective employees (especially if you are a start-up). There again, you have got to know what kind of people you want to hire. There is strong evidence that techies settle down eventually and do all the things that normal people do: marriage, kids, mortgages and stuff. What you as a firm have to decide is who do you want and how are you going to get them (more of this in Chapter 3).

I wouldn't work there for a million

Of course, the other thing we need to keep in mind when we talk about reputation is that although it may be the very, very best, not everyone is going to think so. In recent years we have become obsessed with listing best of breed companies and commenting on how good or bad they are. One thing these lists (like *Fortune* magazine and Harris Interactive) don't take into account is that one man's heaven is another's hell. Perception is all. You don't even have to join them and get the work experience at first hand. Somehow you just know you wouldn't fit in, no matter how bloody good they may be.

Case in point. Hewlett-Packard is always on these lists, mainly because it was a highly profitable and caring organization. The fact that it was full of control freaks all dedicated to the HP way, puts it off limits for a large part of the population it may want to hire from. HP is also a good case for showing why employer branding doesn't work. New CEO Carly Fiorina shook up the company, moved everyone around, refocussed the business and then watched as the discontented packed their bags and walked. The trouble at HP is no-one knows how to perceive it. Who will be happy there and who will not? Now its merger plans with Compaq pose even more problems in working out just what a workplace it will eventually be.

"Best of" polls are fun, because you have to wonder who are the people they ask. In February 2001, Harris Interactive and the Reputation Institute published a corporate reputation poll based on the views of 26,011 respondents. They had six categories to rank reputation:

- emotional appeal;
- products and services;
- workplace environment;
- social responsibility;
- vision and leadership and
- financial performance.

I have a few comments:

Fourth in "emotional appeal" was Fedex. An excellent company, but emotions usually get aroused when your package doesn't arrive. Does putting them into this category as one of the best help their case when Mr Jones calls up and asks where his package has got to? Answer: "No."

In the socially responsible category, Daimler-Chrysler came third. Does announcing mega job cuts count for nought? Maybe 26,011 people think they do a good job, but on the other hand there are 15,000 plus soon to be ex-employees who might just think otherwise. Does this do Daimler-Chrysler's reputation any good? Do they sell more cars because of it? I think not.

Also in this category as a winner is McDonald's. Wow! I spent last summer reading about protests against their omnipresence in the market-place. I even ended up, unwittingly, in the middle of one. Were these protesters hooded anti-capitalists? No. They were concerned mums and dads worried at the arrival of a McDonald's in their midst who see increased traffic flow and litter. Does making the list do them any good? Doubtful, and it won't help them recruit one more hamburger flipper either.

So let's remember that being on these lists is not necessarily a good idea. Also let's not forget that what might suit one person definitely won't do for another. We must be careful when we set out to target people and know who we want.

The danger of smugness

Can you be too good? Possibly. Johnson & Johnson always make these lists, they have a corporate credo that employees actually believe. Some I think must sleep with it framed over their beds. Recently, I have met three relatively senior Johnson & Johnson employees, ALL tell you about the credo (see page 78). The effect is rather like being braced on your front doorstep by some peddler of alternative religion. You think it impolite to slam the door in their face. Having said that, Johnson & Johnson is an excellent company that takes care of its own people and those that it acquires (assuming they go along with the credo). What someone should whisper in the CEO's ear is that there is a danger of slipping into smugness and arrogance. Hey!, there's a new reputation category: The Smuggest Corporations in America.

... and then there's the Chief Executive

Of course highly successful organizations like Johnson & Johnson usually have an excellent roster of top managers who all operate well together and make the firm a successful sum of all its parts. The reputation of firms like these is solid and reassuring, because you know if one of the parts fails the others can carry it along.

Other firms are different. Take one charismatic CEO and it seems that is all you need to make it all work. Prospective employees flock to a firm because it sounds like it might be fun for one reason or another. Engineering company ABB became a talent magnet, because of the reputation of its then CEO Percy Barnevik. The legendary Jack Welsh at General Electric also created a personal perception of an organization that knew where it was going and how it was going to get there.

Low fare airline legend Herb Kelleher built Southwest Airlines on the strength of his own personality. Sure you need people to make it run, but they are attracted by his 21st century pirate image, and his obvious delight in taking on the big boys of the industry and winning. I've used Southwest Airlines employment credo before, and I make no excuses for using it again here (see page 79). Here again is a great example of why we need to know the people we require. The people who will perceive us as a great place to work – a true talent magnet. Jack Welsh isn't going to start an airline, neither are his engineers going to serve drinks on a plane. He wants one thing Herb wants another – the secret is that they know that. The question is do you?

In Europe, low cost airlines are also taking to the skies, but doing things very differently. This very much defines who goes to work where. The son of a Greek shipping tycoon Stelios Haji-Ioannou founded easyJet and made millions. A true entrepreneur, he captured a huge slice of this market by being very visible and now has internet cafés, car rentals and other businesses all in his trade mark ghastly orange color. There is a type of person who works for easyJet, because it has a reputation for taking on the establishment. That perception makes it a talent magnet for certain types of people. However, like Belgium's Orange, how do you switch your image as you become more and more institutionalized?

That's what has happened to Virgin – the brand founded by Richard Branson. It was a great place to work – or perceived to be – by many who saw it as very anti-establishment (taking on British Airways, Coca-Cola, the high street banks, insurance companies and the like). But what happens as your business matures? What happens to the perception when you realize to make an organization like Virgin work, you need – in the reality not the perception – a lot of hard-nosed money men and very professional managers?

When reality strikes

Being a CEO is a dangerous business. According to *Wired* magazine, "45 percent of companies with more than $10 billion in world-wide sales had replaced their CEO in the last three years." And – as most of us old corporate workhorses know – when the boss changes, things change too. So what was a reputation a year ago can quickly be outdated. The other thing that can happen is that the boss gets to believe the reputation, and then things can go sadly wrong.

As marketing guru and Harvard professor Ted Levitt used to love saying, "the companies that fail believed their own bullshit." Well, CEOs are the ones that created it and they often choke on it too.

Here are a few thoughts about CEO reputations and how they can rebound on a business and turn off the talent magnet.

Microsoft may be surging back with great new products, but has it come at a price – in turned off talent. There is no doubt that Bill Gates has a pretty focussed vision and as the Seattle firm became bigger and bigger a lot of the old guard didn't like the new institutionalized atmosphere. As it became more and more successful it acquired the respectability it had for so long shunned. The result? A great deal of top talent left and it became perceived as just another business. Even Gates' obsession with getting his own way was cause for comment. Michael Gartenberg, an IT industry analyst was quoted as saying, "Microsoft is a corporate culture based on four premises: work very hard; Bill is always right; it's us versus them and Bill is always right."

Does this send a good message or a bad one?

Eckhardt Wintzen was a Dutch IT genius who built an amazing organization. Starting in the Netherlands, his Origin group was created on the back of a revolutionary idea. Build up a business and when it gets to 50 people, break it in two. Then do it again and again, until you have a structure that resembles a series of cells. Wintzen toured the globe preaching his "cell theory" from business conference platforms. Meanwhile, Origin's cell-like operation had expanded across Europe and into Asia. The structure gave all the autonomy a certain type of worker loved. Would-be employees flocked to the firm… it was an alternative to a then dominant IBM. These were people who had never owned a white shirt or a tie and were more comfortable in sandals than wing-tips. Salesmen were interviewed in a replica of a Dutch brown café in the company's HQ by Wintzen himself over *maatjes* (raw herrings) and Amstel beer: it was the ultimate cool place to work for those who didn't like the strait-laced, buttoned-down Dutch business culture. It tapped into a talent pool that was just ready for something revolutionary. Then Wintzen sold out – to one of the most staid Dutch corporations, Philips. While it might have been well managed, Philips wasn't a fun place at all, it stood for good Dutch sense and reeked of boredom. Defections followed and Origin took years to finally die, taken over by a French group and now called Atos Origin. But it is a perfect example of how to destroy an image and crucify your reputation. It is also a warning that nothing lasts forever.

Does anyone still remember the Wang Corporation? They were the firm that failed to make the connection between word-processing (which they did) and computing (which IBM and others did). Sometime in the '80s IBM and others ate them for lunch. But in a wonderful example of corporate hubris, I was once asked to organize a tennis match for one of the ruling Wang family in Brussels (then home of their European HQ). We set it up in a private country club. Employees were selected to attend, Wang posted guards and the head honcho appeared. Five employees had been given the great honour of playing Mr Wang at tennis (on the understanding that they let him win). Play commenced. A large bodyguard type, the kind that follows the US President around had posted himself up by the net. He was carrying a smart leather case, rather like the one's that president's aides have for working out the nuclear missile launch codes. Mr Wang played a few sets and then stopped. The bodyguard approached and flipped open the locks on the case. A new product we thought. Maybe a portable word processor, we imagined (hey, this was the early '80s). Not to be. Mr Wang stuck his hand in the case and came out with a can of Coke, which dripped condensation. This case was a drinks cooler! And he didn't offer any of us a slurp. What's the message when the employees who witness this go back to Euro-HQ? Guess, why don't you.

Think that's weird? I was also there the day Harold Geneen, the legendary manager who built ITT into the world's largest conglomerate finally flipped and let it show. Harold had been born in Brighton, England – emigrating to the USA early in life. However, he developed a strange attachment to cricket – not a game well known in either the New York or Brussels headquarters from which he operated. On one trip, on the way back from Brussels to New York he had the corporate jet – a great big Boeing thing – diverted, with all the VPs on board to stop-off in England for a village cricket match. The cost of keeping some of America's corporate finest sitting on the grass watching an incomprehensible game and drinking warm beer can only be imagined. Ah, but I'm not through yet. Seeing that Harold was truly smitten by the seductive noise of leather on wood, the most senior executives decided to give him a surprise. By secretly visiting his New York tailor they got his clothing sizes and proceeded to have an entire cricket outfit created for him, right down to the little striped cap and the massive leather leg pads. They could have, of course, chosen to give him his gift at some private ceremony in an executive dining room, but no. Someone decided that this was too good an opportunity to miss. So to the bemusement of local employees (who know as much about cricket as your average Martian), they created a photo session in the massive lobby of the ITT tower at the top end of Avenue Louise in Brussels. There Harold, happily going along with all this, solemnly (I am not making this up) kitted himself out in the full regalia of an English test match cricketer. For those who witnessed this it was an unforgettable moment. That's when they decided Harold was just slightly out of touch with reality and it was the day they figured it was time to look to pastures new.

Reputation says it all and surveys support the theory

A survey by the Corporate Leadership Council proves beyond much doubt that the firm's reputation and that of the CEO are paramount in attracting and retaining talent.

Using a one to five scorecard (five high), they discovered that the boss thing rules the work environment.

Boss reputation	4.74
Recognition	3.94
Empowerment	3.71
Co-worker reputation	3.68
Work challenge	3.48
Cutting-edge work	3.36

In the organizational environment category reputation also came first, second and third:

Company reputation	3.69
Development reputation	3.56
Senior team reputation	3.50
Technology	3.39
Risk-taking	3.15

A good example here is Federal Express. Founder and CEO, Fred Smith has a great reputation and it is not only hard earned but he makes sure that he works at it. At Fedex, people are important and he wants to stress that message. All managers, worldwide, go through the manager's induction process in Memphis, and Smith makes sure that he attends every one (I understand he has done this once every two weeks or so, for the past 20 years). This is a way to build a reputation that you care about your people enough to spend real time with them.

Our own survey by the American Management Association's M-World also looked at reputation. "Why", we asked, "do you think that people are attracted to a certain corporation?"

The overall reputation of the firm	74%
The reputation of an individual manager	28%
The reputation of a division	13%
The reputation of a department	10%

So you can see that individual manager's do count. And in organizations with a lot of personal autonomy you will see a manager's ability to make things happen becomes a real attractor. I recently worked for a business where one division was clearly in crisis and the other the complete opposite. Most of it came down to the actions of individual managers. Prior to Christmas, the headquarters sent out an e-mail to all managers saying that due to the current austerity program there would be no staff Christmas parties. The manager of the successful division, enlarged the size of the message to massive proportions and made copies which he posted all over the building, with the word, "bullshit, we're having one anyway!" scrawled across it. They did, the manager paid for it, everyone loved him and he loved his performance bonus! In the process he created a team that would walk through fire for him.

When we asked the subscribers of M-World to help us, we asked them a few other questions: here are some responses that may make you think a little more about reputations, why you need one and what sort you should have. It is also a good indication of what this group (aged around 25–35) see as their work expectations and priorities. You should ask yourself if your business has these and if not should you be providing this kind of working climate?

We asked them if they liked the company they worked for, what were the real turn-ons in the reputation that makes them want to stay.

Here's a selection:

- open to alternative lifestyles;
- strong emphasis on customer service and loyalty;
- fun place, good people and great management philosophies;
- employees are treated as valued assets of the business;
- career boosting, professional demeanor at every level of the business;
- they love to create fun work environments for people;
- open working conditions, work on new and exciting projects;
- they are about challenges and fulfilling your potential;
- ability to change jobs/career without leaving company;
- they want you to be successful in business and personal life;
- they stretch one's talent to the limit;
- it's a teenage GE that is aggressive in building a strategic business;
- they empower employees to make big decisions themselves.

Then we asked the M-Word group to tell us who they would not like to work for. I decided the legal risks were too great, especially when we asked for specifics! However, a few non-attributable comments will get you into the right frame of mind:

- large impersonal conglomerates who think they're cool;
- airlines, they have a volatile environment with minimal job security;
- almost any retail company;
- I work for the government and it has to be the worst;
- any company without innovative ideas;
- most start-ups;
- any company that always stress and make decisions based on the bottom line only.

Following on, we asked if they didn't like the business they worked for why were they looking to move. These answers are a guide to how to destroy your reputation. However, I believe that everyone who reads them will find at least one item that will make you shudder and your spine tingle. You'll be thinking "we do that.!"

- bad communication to employees. HR practices treat employees liked numbers, not people;
- the burn out rate is high (I should know, I've been there!);
- they are unable to deal effectively with the diverse population within the company;
- they're too full of themselves to see how others view them;
- poor hours, poor salary, poor work conditions, standing for hours;
- they have many double standards when it comes to growth and advancement;
- they keep repeating the same mistakes;
- they request competencies they don't require. In fact they demoralize;
- top down hierarchies. Employees are interchangeable part numbers;
- they depend so much on buyers that they serve buyers better than the employees;
- promotions are based on favoritism and nepotism;
- the company has now matured and has lost its capability to live.

And I got this (and I did take out the name of the firm, although this is now on the internet doing great things for the company's reputation!).

"Company X has supervisors that treat people very poorly. They yell and scream at people and demean them in many ways. They expect all managers to work 24 hours a day with no 'thank you.' Employee communications are punitive and threatening. The message from the very top of the organization is that employees are easily expendable and should be happy just to have a job. At the same time they tell employees that they are a family-oriented organization and that employees are their greatest resource. They don't know how to begin to walk-the-talk."

Guess we'll just have to rush round there and sign up for a bit of abuse!

Recognizing bad organizations

A namesake of mine, wrote a book recently, titled *Workaholism: Getting a Life in the Killing Fields of Work*. It's worth a read, if that is the kind of worry that concerns you about your employees. In the book, he and co-author, Paul Thorne have a list of what the bad organization does. In terms of doing anything for reputation it stinks, but, again, you'd better see if any of your organization's practices are here.

Internal communication in my organization…

- seems to encourage people to keep secrets and tell lies rather than open up;
- often gives mixed or conflicting messages that leave me confused as to what was really meant;
- gives equal prominence to trivia and important messages;
- requires me to work hard if I want to find out what's really going on;
- is mostly gossip.

Decisions are made in my company…

- apparently without any recall of the past, so that mistakes are often repeated;
- usually better when there is a crisis;
- From a narrow set of options, limiting the choices that could be made;

- quickly, because judgements tend to be black and white;
- in a way that can often seem very detached from the real world.

The accepted rules of successful behaviour in my organization are …

- conflict must not be brought into the open, but kept hidden and suppressed;
- always make sure that someone else gets the blame;
- keep your feelings to yourself;
- in excusing non-delivery, start the explanation with, "if only" and "if it weren't for;"
- treat colleagues as a means of getting things done, not as people.

A reputation is also about living values

There are organizations that try hard, even in adversity. Also there are CEOs who understand the "people thing" and are determined not to leave that to others. There may not be many but there are some. In showing that concern, they raise the perception of their organization as a place where – some of us, at least – might want to park our *derrières* for a while.

Possibly the best example that exists today (although as their profits slip, we'll have to wait and see) is Finnish mobile phone maker Nokia. Jorma Ollila, the CEO believes that the people stuff is actually HIS responsibility. "As a CEO," he says, "I have two tasks. I am the HR manager for my company and I am the top salesman for my company. My time is really shared between these two things."

How refreshing! Can we have a few more good men (and women) like Jorma please?

This is a company where the CEO decided he didn't want to get any bigger. As they hit 50,000 employees (60% outside Finland) he, "put in place active programs to ensure that we wouldn't grow in terms of personnel anymore. I don't want to be CEO of 100,000 people."

The reason that Jorma believes Nokia has been able to get its business right so far – and maintain itself as a beacon for talent – is the strong presense of values set deep within the business. Jorma explains: "Values are extremely important to the youngsters of our era and at Nokia, values hold our global organization together: they act as our glue." Think about your company and what you have to do.

Nokia's CEO says that in their business, "The Nokia way is a feedback loop that incorporates culture, values, attitudes and management behavior." The values of that loop, as set by the firm, are: customer satisfaction; respect for the individual; achievement and continuous learning.

But Nokia and its HR-involved CEO don't stop there. According to the firm's view, sticking on the labels is just the beginning. "How you implement those values is 90 percent of it," says Jorma Ollila, "there has to be a distinct correlation between the values and how your people see the company to be."

That is exactly what we have been talking about throughout this chapter: it doesn't matter what you Mr Manager think, it's what perception your employees and prospective employees have of you that counts.

Others do the same

In their own special way, other companies are out there in the market building, or rebuilding, a reputation too. The one thing they have in common is that everyone is doing it for their own needs and their own reasons.

Siemens, as we saw earlier, has totally remodeled itself totally for one simple reason – it had to. It couldn't recruit the people it wanted – it's employer brand was seriously out-of-date and unfocussed on future business needs. As their recruiting initiative says, "to improve Siemens recognition on the international labor market as a global employer of choice and therefore improve our ability to: attract; select; integrate and retain the right talent." Quietly, not with too much fanfare they have achieved that.

Manpower needs to be known as more than the company you call when your secretary goes sick. Moreover, it needs to recruit its own high quality talent. Until now the image was wrong. Working full-time for a temporary services company didn't send the right message – the right perception. Manpower has now reinvented itself... or so it says. CEO, Jeff Joerres has gone public saying that, "People Knowledge and Innovation are the three most important elements that bind us together as a global company with one global identity. They are the three things that make us Manpower. I challenge you to live by these Values every day in your work. I promise I will do the same."

In Denmark, innovation is burgeoning in getting the right rep in the marketplace. In a country where liberal employee policies are practically the norm, getting your reputation right and keeping it is a – well let's say – low key race. Engineering company Unimerco has ping-pong tables between the desks and a gourmet restaurant plus a 24-hour bakery (yes, hours are very flexible!). Elsewhere, software firm DMZ has the ultimate perk for the struggling code-writer, the company dog that lives at reception and takes stressed employees for walks in the forest behind the facility. DMZ also have free Carlsberg beer on tap from pour-your-own drinking fountains in the corridors (try that one Silicon Valley!).

Of course, occasionally the wheels come off the project and it skids into the crash barriers. Sweden's IKEA – the butt of all those flat-pack furniture jokes – decided that it would share out all the money its customers poneyed up on one day. This meant that everyone from Beijing to Baltimore to Brussels, would get the same amount, no matter how senior you were. Sadly, things went a little awry, as the firm – who have evangelistic managers who insist on flying coach and stay in two-star hotels when they travel – realized that tax implications across a host of countries would create serious problems for its 40,000 workers. A spokesman at the time said, "Ingvar Kamprad (the founder of IKEA) has always found his own way of doing business and rewarding workers." This time it was a flat pack too far. But the reputation held.

... then, of course you can try and change in adversity

As I have already pointed out, big, global businesses can have a good reputation in one place and a lousy one in another. Similarly, they can be in trouble with a plummeting stock price and a massive redundancy program and still be doing good things. That is the nature of business in the 21st Century. Later I'll look at some of the options, but here are three companies who know what it means to be trying to pedal in two directions at once. You need to be attractive but a lot of people hate you too.

We've already highlighted Motorola as a troubled organization with a long-term lay-off strategy, yet it is still trying to hire as well. Getting it's name out as a place of innovation and a place where people can learn becomes an ongoing challenge, that must be accomplished.

Zurich Financial Services are another firm that hit the rocks – hard. Share price suffered and people started to be let go. However, it is fighting to find a new renaissance and still gather in new people to help it refocus. Much of that has gone into better communication and a more transparent view of what its plans for the future are. It launched a "communications leadership" initiative, designed to take the company forward and help restore and enervate its reputation in the marketplace. That initiative was based on moving the way they communicated from:

passive	to	engaged
closed/static	to	smart
slow	to	alert
machine-like	to	responsive
one-way	to	interactive
hierarchical	to	relevant
predetermined	to	community building
compartmentalized	to	shared

Apparel maker, Levi Strauss garnered terrible press with some high profile workplace cases brought by employees. That, allied to factory closures, made the one time icon of West Coast companies a bad bet for exuding corporate charisma. Using their employees as the base they set out to change that, creating a program called "Partners in Performance" that was intended to address the reputation issues head on. The program is founded on eight principles:

- bring company aspirations to life;
- create a single system for salaried employees;
- link employees more tightly to business strategy;
- increase emphasis on performance-based pay;
- reward individual contribution to team success;
- maintain the competitive position of the company;
- improve performance management;
- improve communications.

It may not be revolutionary, but it does get people inside and outside developing the perception that they care about what they are doing, and that without a reputation you are not going to get very far these days.

The value of volunteer and sponsor programs

Another way that you can get a good reputation is to involve your employees in volunteer programs. Socially or community-conscious employees find this type of commitment by the company a very acceptable way for big business to do something for others – and they, your employees, are directly involved. While this sort of activity may not actually get you many people in terms of active hiring, it does help in the retention process.

Then again, you can also get the attention of the employee by backing useful culture projects – especially if you can find a way to involve them. Even if it is the hobby of your chairman, sponsoring an art show or something similar will get noticed and may well help in the recruitment process. Anyway, it is another thing to think about.

.... and finally

If you want the right people to do the job you have to learn to appeal not only to their needs but give them a feeling that they will be totally and unequivocally welcome in your business. Here's the *Wall Street Journal*'s take on this:

> In an unusually tight job market employers everywhere are searching for new hiring tactics. For the first time, major Wall Street financial institutions are targeting recruitment efforts at gay and lesbian business students. At [bankers] J.P. Morgan, gay employees formed Gleam (Gay and Lesbian Employees at Morgan) to make hiring processes more welcoming for gay recruits. Goldman Sachs and Merrill Lynch are also forming networks with the goal of mobilizing and attracting gay workers.

Why are these firms, plus American Express and McKinsey doing it? To raise the perception that gay men and women are not only welcome but valued at these organizations.

As we move on to other issues, it is important to realize that the reputation of a business isn't a singular thing. It is many and very fragmented. Keeping those many reputations polished and relevant is a task that begins with the CEO and is promoted and projected by every employee, customer and supplier.

ONE CREDO, ONE CHARTER FOR FREEDOM

Johnson & Johnson are justly proud of their credo, which they live by every day. Rumor has it that keen employees have it framed over their beds! It is – in this glitzy world – a bit old fashioned, but it works for them and it also reflects the kind of employees who respond to that, who perceive the firm in a certain light and want to work for it. Southwest Airlines is a whole lot of alternative lifestyle. As I have talked about flexibility and freedom, this is the credo to die for if you are that type of person. Two organizations with two very different approaches, both magnets for the type of talent they need.

Johnson & Johnson

Johnson & Johnson scores high on all the reputation lists. Its proudest asset is the credo that was developed years ago and is still revered by employees today. Unlike other organizations with the mission statement hidden in a desk drawer, this – say employees – is what they live by every day. Their reputation, if you like, hangs on this. Whether it would make you beat a path to their door or not, it is worth, in a discussion about reputations, to consider how many of the companies that we work for could live up to this. Like it or not, it works for them.

Our Credo

We believe our first responsibility is to the doctors, nurses and patients, to mothers and fathers and all others who use our products and services. In meeting their needs everything we do must be of high quality. We must constantly strive to reduce our costs in order to maintain reasonable prices. Customers' orders must be serviced promptly and accurately. Our suppliers and distributors must have an opportunity to make a fair profit.

We are responsible to our employees, the men and women who work with us throughout the world. Everyone must be considered an individual. We must respect their dignity and recognize their merit. They must have a sense of security in their jobs. Compensation must be fair and adequate, and working conditions clean, orderly and safe. We must be mindful of ways to help our employees fulfill their family responsibilities. Employees must feel free to make suggestions and complaints. There must be equal opportunity of employment, development and advancement for those qualified. We must provide competent management, and their actions must be just and ethical.

We are responsible to the communities in which we live and work and to the world community as well. We must be good citizens – support good works and charities and bear our fair share of taxes. We must encourage civic improvements and better health and education. We must maintain in good order the property we are privileged to use, protecting the environment and natural resources.

Our final responsibility is to our stockholders. Business must make a sound profit. We must experiment with new ideas. Research must be carried on, innovative programs developed and mistakes paid for. New equipment must be purchased, new facilities provided and new products launched. Reserves must be created to provide for adverse times. When we operate according to these principles, the stockholders should realize a fair return.

It may have the echo of the '30s in the words, but it works for them. The question is would it work for you and what would you perceive their reputation to be and what kind of a place to work would it be?

Southwest Airlines

Southwest Airlines Freedom Charter

Dallas-based Southwest Airlines is known for its excessively happy employees and delighted customers. Zany tactics, like telling jokes in-flight, pay off in a firm where fun comes first, second and third. What might be not so well known is the airline's employee charter, which is a serious bill of rights wrapped up in a candy bar. How many other companies would dare adopt it? But it gives the right image, the right reputation and the right perception of what they want to be and who they want to attract.

We believe that all people of Southwest Airlines have unalienable rights to life, liberty and the pursuit of happiness with a passion and reckless abandon never anticipated by the founding fathers. We hereby dedicate our hearts and minds to create: ➜

- Freedom to earn through shared efforts to free the people of the United States of America to roam about the country making new friends, eating excessive holiday dinners, participating in sporting events beyond their physical capacities and connecting with people and experiences that make the world bigger and brighter.

- Freedom to learn how to change software, tires, diapers, investments, elections, our minds and other important stuff that allows us to do the best work of our careers and take on personal challenges that mere mortals would never attempt. (And, yes, we will try this at home.)

- Financial freedom to buy cars, homes, stereos, college educations, comfortable retirement accommodation, insurances and really great pizza with lots of extra cheese (but no anchovies).

- Freedom to live, take road trips, coach Little League, hang out with our kids, go to school, be weekend warriors of the courts and fields, do the culture thing, take sabbaticals and give back to our communities.

- Freedom to be healthy, happy, eat tofu, yogurt and those little nuts that taste like tree bark, join great health plans, visit awesome doctors and protect our family's health and well-being.

- Freedom to roam about the country celebrating the value of travel in our lives by using travel to learn, strengthen relationships, renew our souls, connect with loved ones, see the world and yes… to seek out great shopping.

- Freedom to have fun, be ourselves, and spread laughter, humor and the Southwest spirit of freedom (but no airline food) across the good old US of A.

Like Johnson & Johnson's credo, Southwest Airline employees believe in it and live it every day.

And let's not forget that this is not a perfect world. I am sure there are many who join out of curiosity and recoil in horror as it just isn't for them.

3 | Talent magnetism: people, places, and ... er pets

> We've all been blessed with God-given talents.
> Mine just happens to be beating people up.
>
> SUGAR RAY LEONARD

> If you want to attract top talent to an old-line city
> like Cleveland, wait until it's warm. Ice storms are
> the ultimate turn-off for knowledge workers.
>
> STEPHEN HARDIS, EATON CORPORATION

No such thing as long-term planning?

I am sitting in a room in mid-2001 with a trio of very, very senior human resource people. These three are so "with it" they probably don't even consider themselves HR people anymore. Anyway they aren't really HR people, never have been. They are as far away from the cares and woes of the personnel department as you can get. They've never seen a payroll print-out, never worried over a pension plan. These guys are hired for one thing alone: to worry about talent. Why don't we have enough? Who are we losing it to? How do we get more? For anyone who thinks that HR people don't think strategically you should meet this lot – they're scary! One is an ex-banker for goodness sake!, and ex-oilman and a former heavy-hitter in fast moving consumer goods (FMCG). They all get very well paid – with bonuses too – to think about five years ahead. No such thing as long-term planning? Ha! of course there is.

These three all have the ear and the private mobile phone code for the chairman. They represent between them over $150 billion and more than

300,000 employees. Still, they struggle to get talent to turn up and then to stick.

What concerns these guys, possibly three of the most powerful talent procurers on earth?

- The banker: I have 250 highly talented individuals, all under 35 and all worth more than $10 million. My big concern, how long can I expect them to commute to work everyday and, when they decide to stay home, where do the next generation come from?

- The oilman: Our organization is suffering from a talent famine. Big oil isn't a place to build a career anymore and it is showing. We've always grown our own timber from college graduate to vice-president. We can't do that anymore, the industry isn't cool, isn't fun and just doesn't appeal.

- The FMCG man: Globalization led to a loss of talent for us rather than the reverse. Our product strategy was developed, imposed and measured from headquarters, so bright young marketers quit and joined other industries. Our concern is to reverse this trend and appeal to a new generation.

As part of beginning to understand some of the people issues we are all facing in creating and sustaining our firms as talent magnets, let's look in a little more detail at what this trio of outstanding talent developers is going to have to do to get their firms back on track. At the same time, let's weave in a few comments, insights and advice by others in their industry on what it is going to take to make it all work.

Bankers

Bankers have problems. One of the most pressing is that they have made a lot of fairly young talented people seriously rich. If you are sitting on a lotta loot, are you really going to want to get in the office before nine in the morning and do your stuff. Does a dirty subway commute appeal?

The answer, of course is "no." That's why every major bank is beginning to put together wider and wider talent searches. Searches that are taking them from the traditional recruiting grounds of the top business schools to a second tier of countries. Banks I have spoken to are putting newly graduated talent from Poland, Portugal, Macao, Brazil and Russia onto fast-track learning programs. The idea is that they need to look deeper and further than before. If they cannot do that they will, literally, run out of talent to fuel their business objectives. Furthermore, bankers will have to spend a lot more time "stroking" the best talent they already have. As one banker told me, "My job is to make sure that the top people who work for me know that this IS the very best place they can work. They have to take home with them every night the idea that they are in the very best organization on earth, that gives them the very best challenges and pays them better – or equal to anything they can get on the outside. The day we burst that bubble is the day we have lost." Similarly, a former Citicorp senior executive once said to me, "yes, we drive them [our high potentials] very hard. But you need to consider that when they get a country of their own to manage they are possibly going to be the most important person in it apart from the Prime Minister or the president, and basically, that's because we've secured his loans he owes us money!" Now that's a talent magnet, not for everyone, but for a lot of the people you need. It's all about challenge, with a good dollop of ego thrown in for good measure.

So how do you, in the banking or financial services world get set to be a talent magnet in the 21st century?

- make it your mission to look for high potential talent in places you have never looked before;

- have a program that gets your firm noticed by those you want to influence (local business schools, industry groups etc);

- have a high profile award, prize or other sponsorship initiative that garners you focussed, rifle shot publicity amongst the potential candidate group;

- manage the hell out of them so they realize that this is something they won't get anywhere else;

- keep the learning curve steep and very varied;

- hold their interest by getting them to use their skills in "out of bank" events, committees and think tanks;

- think long and hard about how you change the culture of your "institution." Many managers want to find ways of working from home but won't due to peer pressure. How do you get around that?

- Where you are seeking to have and hold high-performance specialists be prepared – as some banks have already done – to have professional managers that do the "people" stuff for the experts and team leaders.

Oil and gas

The oil and gas industry is having a hard time too. Basically it has a credibility problem with younger graduates, who see its record in the environmental area as well as its profitability as unacceptable. While they don't totally shun it they don't see it as a place for them. This is causing problems for many of the big majors who have traditionally hired graduates straight from college and then waved them goodbye at 60, managing their career all the way. Simply put, this doesn't work anymore, but, to date, most oil firms haven't managed to find very much of a useful solution. Senior managers headhunted from other industries have rarely lasted long. In an industry not noted for its talent churn this is unsettling. However, there is no doubt that a shortage of talent internally and the difficulty of getting mid-career hires to stick is going to have to be addressed – and soon.

One other issue compounding the problem is mobility – or rather lack of it. In the good old, bad old days a manager basically got told to go home and tell his wife (it was always a wife) that they were off to Brazil for three years. That was all part of the career you signed up for. Today, the still mostly male managers have wives who work and won't move. They in turn refuse too.

So the issues that need addressing with some urgency if they are to recover their once highly respected reputation as magnets for talent are:

- a less than sexy image;
- a shrinking internal, old-guard talent pool;
- limits to mobility.

What to do?

- a massive diversity program needs to be put in place to hire from (like the bankers) non-traditional areas and countries. This includes hiring women, who still don't figure in many big oil hierarchies except at the fringes of power;

- a communications' program aimed specifically at soon-to-graduate talent to show that the industry is changing and can offer exciting, challenging work. In other terms "you gotta get sexy;"

- a more focussed approach to promoting earlier and pressing talented employees to want to become managers;

- equally, an understanding that there is a great deal of talent that doesn't want people responsibilities, these people need to be put on other, lucrative development tracks that utilize, not squander, their skills;

- a careful program of external recruitment, that doesn't just plug gaps but aims to not only hire but fully orients mid and senior level recruits into the business to fully embrace the culture.

FMCG

The FMCG industry has its share of woes too. Dominated, like big oil, by big players – who traditionally stole talent from each other – they have all found themselves under siege as other industries have realized where marketing talent was located. Procter and Gamble, Unilever, Nestlé and Sara Lee have all suffered badly at the hands of predatory head-hunters stealing their people for other industries that need the branding skills that FMCG professionals have.

What to do?

- it doesn't look as though the FMCG industry is going to stop haemorrhaging skilled executives any time soon, so the imperative must be to both cast the search net wider and be prepared to bring on more high potentials through a more intensive identification and development program;

- again, they are going to have to dig deeper for graduates and make them realize that a career in an FMCG company can be both rewarding, stimulating and fun;

- they may well have to consider the locations some of them operate from and be prepared to move key functional areas or the headquarters of business units to places where top talent wants to live;

- they will have to learn to promote people ("taking on the risk") faster than today, otherwise high potentials will jump for better offers;

- they will need to consider that (like big oil) hiring in mid-to-senior level people from outside the industry can be a good thing if it is managed in the right way.

SUBSTANTIAL HELP

Cleveland, Ohio's Able-One's Moving, is so desperate for talent that it hires workers, with substance-abuse problems and then helps them by referring them to Alcoholics Anonymous.

A laundry-list of worries

If those are some of the options that finance houses, oil companies and FMCG firms can consider, what's on the agenda that they have to concern themselves with? What are the issues and initiatives that keep our three human capital gurus awake at night?

While some things are highly focussed on a specific industry's requirements, the real concerns are remarkably similar. Below is the laundry list that – I imagine – any senior HR man or woman must have in their top pocket and look at every day.

The Human Capital Laundry List of Issues, Needs and Expectations: (in no particular order of importance)

Diversity programs

Organizations must get better – quickly – at being able to comfortably manage a wide range of personnel from different social, religious and cultural backgrounds. The majority of major corporations are dominated – not just at the top – by white male managers. This needs to change. Diversity also includes women and minorities. If we don't begin to do this as a matter of course, just part of business as usual, we are, in effect, managing under a policy where we deliberately restrict access to vast pools of highly competent talent. The other factor is that we are, more and more, hiring people who don't really belong in our business. Or at least they didn't used to. We have people whose cultural touch-points are very different from those of our industry. For example, insurers employ geologists, meteorologists and physicists to counsel them on earthquakes and other natural disasters and weather patterns; banks have academics versed in chaos theory and the like. Managing these people opens up a whole new set of challenges for our industries.

Work/life balance

Buzz-phrase or major concern? There is little doubt that work/life balance (of which a lot more in Chapter 5) is something that concerns employees. In most firms it is all about how to live a life dominated by a long-hours culture, excessive business travel, long commutes and juggling children and social life as well. Certainly employees working in fast-paced firms, who have little time out of work appreciate concierge systems (like laundry video rental and supermarket services), a nanny-at-home service for sick kids as well as at work gyms and massage opportunities. However, there seems little doubt that organizations must take a clear stand on this and develop policies that are meaningful and are clearly understood. Addressing work/life balance issues on an *ad hoc*, case-by-case basis seems to send the wrong messages, create petty jealousies and is a recipe for eventual organizational chaos.

In my view, organizations must set a policy and stick to it – however tough or tender it might be – so employees know where they stand. If you are going to have sabbaticals, then set a policy and say so. If you don't want them in your business, make that clear too. If employees are pushing to exchange salary for days off, decide if you can afford to do this in terms of the disruption it will cause. You can have corporate guidelines, but remember – especially if you are an international organization – that local managers need to use their own discretion. What would be welcome in one country or region, won't be even understood or appreciated in another.

Telecommuting

This can be regarded as part of the work/life balance debate, but it could also be viewed as a stand-alone issue. Firms need to make a clear decision about what role telecommuting should play in their business. This can range from equipping employees with home offices, to doling out a mobile phone and a laptop. Again, failure to take into account everyone's needs can cause problems. Simple things like answering the phone of a part-time telecommuter when they are out of the office can create all sorts of issues. Equally, some people are completely unsuited to this type of work, needing on-site supervision. And there are jobs like that too. So, get a policy and fine-tune it as you develop it. That's if you want to have it at all.

Pensions and other benefits

These still seem to be concerns of employees – particularly those that are planning to stay. While most pensions are fully portable these days there is also a major move for firms to limit funding or leave these kinds of provisions to individuals to work out. However, there is no doubt that pension-style benefits and major health cover are on the agenda of most professional managers, who – if they are going to stay with you – expect it to cover the rest of their immediate family. Equally, in some countries (UK and the USA come quickly to mind) many families opt for fee-paying schools and are looking to their employers to assist. Again, unless you want an HR operation that is all over the place, policies need to be clear and unambiguous. Incidentally, most companies miss out on the opportunity to let them know just how much they do give them in addition to salary. Hoescht Celanese, showed every employee just how much was invested in them in addition to salary – figuring rightly that few had a clue. They explained the value of pensions, health care, cars and other perks: retention levels rose by over 40 percent. Try it, it's easy to do and doesn't cost much either.

Professional and personal development

This has to be a key part of human resource strategy. Today, everyone puts professional and personal development at the very top of the list of "needs" they expect employers to fulfill. But it's a lot more complex than that. Specific groups need very careful attention. High performers in all disciplines need their own process, so too do future general managers. Being known for offering the very best in training and development becomes a major attractor – don't stint on it. It can – when done right – save you a bundle of recruiting dollars and boost retention.

Tracking ex-employees and re-hiring strategies

Remember the days when you left a company and you went on their blacklist – never to be re-hired under any circumstances? Ah, how times have changed! Today, smart organizations are actively keeping in touch with ex-employees (it can be as simple as mailing them a Christmas card or a company diary every year). Ex-employees – well, the ones you didn't fire for some unspeakable act! – are really worth seeking out – they know the business, have usually learned a lot since they left you and will quickly and seamlessly integrate. Some organizations are making this a major initiative, one even has an ex-employees newsletter which they mail out every month. Especially in an innovative company, getting an ex-employees attention can be all it takes for them to pick up the phone. Why? Because they probably left to go and pursue some new idea, technology or product, so if they find out that you have some new challenges they'll want to be a part of it.

Communications

No matter how much organizations seem to spend, they never spend enough. Always at the top of the "you could do better" section of employee attitude surveys, communication has never ever had much of an easy ride in any business. One of the first things to be axed in a downturn, it is also one of the organizational orphans (or poisoned chalices), never seeming to find a home. Communication gets run by the CEO's office, marketing, HR, finance, depending on the focus of the business. But, as everyone knows (but does little about) communication needs attention. As we employ more and more intelligent people, we have to keep them informed. If we don't, they find out anyway. I am not sure just how many alternative corporate websites there are these days, but if you want to know all the dirt on the business you work for – or are thinking of working for – then a few key strokes will take you there. Somehow, top management don't seem to have understood that too well, but it is a fact of life. We owe it to the people who work for us to keep them aware about what our plans are and we owe it to our employees to allow them to feedback to us what they think. The biggest problem with communication is that most employees don't believe what top management say half the time. Just as reputation management (as I described in Chapter 2) is going to need a lot more time and money spent on it, so too will communications. And, if you can, don't give it to some fresh-faced kid, get a seasoned employee who knows the business. This will be a hard sell though, no-one in my experience ever made vice-president or partner by having responsibility for internal communications on their job description!

Funding incubator firms

This is another, new, but key issue. It is also quite an emotive one. However, companies are finding out that if they want to keep some of their top talent, it might be better to give them the funds to build a start-up, than letting them go elsewhere and do it. Equally, getting a reputation for being innovative and supportive in this way sends a great message to the outside world and really acts as a talent magnet. It probably depends on your business whether or not you can consider it. Then again, if you want to attract and retain innovative people, maybe it is just a question of stretching their and your imaginations. Doing this as a knee-jerk reaction to a threat of people leaving possibly isn't a great idea. But, like so much else in having and holding talent, flexibility needs to be there.

Attracting the next generation

Making sure that the Twinkies of today are your high performers (Hipo's) of tomorrow is paramount. As we have already seen, for many it is difficult. Firms are going to have to spend a lot more time and money on getting their case across to the next generation if they are to secure a plentiful supply of new talent. This means that they are going to have to change their perception in the marketplace. For some, this is going to be hard work and will mean tearing down a lot of very sacred cultural icons that have served them well for many years. However, it would seem that many of the dinosaurs of the past will have to reinvent themselves if they are to successfully compete for talent on the global market. Today, there are a lot of "cool" places for talent to work, whose talent magnet is far, far stronger. Neither do I think that this can be solved by a slick advertising campaign. This is a long-term battle that needs to be won. It isn't over in months or years, it will be an ongoing fight to be a better talent magnet than not only your direct competition but other industries as well. The place to start? Try and understand what those Twinkies want in a job, a career, a life. If you aren't tuned into that, you can't begin to prepare yourself for the fight. My suggestion? If your top management can't accept the need to change – go work for someone who does!

BUGGED TALENT

Onel de Guzman, the high-school drop-out who created the Love Bug virus that went around the world was deluged with offers of jobs from the very firms his virus invaded. "They see me as a talent that can help them in the future," Onel told reporters.

So what does the talent want?

Talent, I am convinced, comes in all shapes and sizes. We cannot just talk of top talent because we can never have enough of it and we never will. What we have to realize is that in this search to be a talent magnet, we are going to, hopefully, get the interest of some real heavy-hitters. But, to be honest, most of the talent is going to be of the mundane, run-of-the-mill variety. Learning to attract that and manage it well is going to be key. Whether top-top talent, or fairly mediocre, we had better know what they expect, otherwise it is pretty difficult to bait the hook.

A recent Dutch study of employee expectations says it all – well almost. Over 7,000 Dutch businessmen and women were asked the question, "Why do you stay with your current employer?" Here are their responses:

I have an interesting job	87%
I have possibilities for growth	78%
I like my colleagues	55%
The responsibility of the job	47%
I have a good salary	41%
I get good development	40%

A similar survey of almost 2,000 employees by HR consultants Towers Perrin in the USA sought to separate how people felt their needs were actually being met by their employers. This is how they rated organizational performance:

	Level of need	Need being met by employer
Satisfying/challenging work	84%	59%
Competitive base salary	84%	52%
Effective leadership	76%	41%
Advancement opportunities	72%	42%
Training programs	72%	48%
Performance feedback		
And coaching	71%	42%
Developmental assignments	70%	47%
Recognition programs	53%	36%

I suppose I can stop writing now. If we cannot get some of these basic, the-kind-everyone-knows-about-needs, right, how can we ever begin to think about becoming a talent magnet? There are a lot more of these surveys by McKinsey, Boston Consulting Group, Cap Gemini Ernst & Young, PriceWaterhouseCoopers. They all say the same thing: the gap between employee expectation and reality is getting wider and we seem hell bent on doing bugger-all about it. Why? Are we just too busy? Do we think about people issues last thing on a Friday when all the fires that we faced on Monday morning are finally out?

Certainly, these studies have shown that there is little sympathy for the people issues by chief executives as a collective group (see Chapter 7), but surely someone somewhere is doing something? Maybe they are and not telling the employees about it.

Commenting on his survey, Towers Perrin's Richard Meischeid had this to say, "What's interesting here is that the areas where employees feel the most dissatisfied are those we define as non-traditional rewards. This is consistent with a growing body of research showing that things like leadership, development, advancement and work challenge are increasingly important to employees, especially the highly skilled. Employers who fail to focus on these areas may well find themselves at a competitive disadvantage in recruiting and retention."

I've news for you Dick, they already are at a disadvantage, but many don't yet know it, or aren't willing to admit it. By the time someone gets the news through to the executive corridors of power it will be too late.

Here's a line from a McKinsey view in the Economist Intelligence Unit's, *Strategic Finance*. "Talented professionals dislike being managed. To make matters more difficult, management has to manage a group of talented people whose interests, backgrounds and skills may be quite different, but who share a strong aversion to being managed." They continue: "Talented individuals want the space to get on with their jobs as they see fit. They hate layers of management and bureaucracy. With few exceptions, they do not believe in budgeting – you can hardly forecast next week's revenues, let alone produce a five-year plan that will prove accurate. They loathe meetings and internal memoranda, especially planning documents, go straight in the trash. Thus the traditional levels of command and control management structures simply do not work for them."

And why? Because employees and prospective employees want different stuff from the smart-suited chaps who run our global empires. Can someone volunteer to tell them or have the last ten messengers been summarily shot for giving out what they see as bad news in the boardroom? Somehow, we are going to have to convince top management that the world has buzzed around a few revolutions since they were junior managers. People want a life outside work too, and they are going to get it one way or another.

Look at these examples and you'll begin to see how today's youth thinks.

Chip-maker Intel Corporation was surprised to learn that prospective recruits at California State University had been discussing the parking lot at Intel's Folsom facility. Noting that the lot is full until late into the evening, some had concluded that long work hours are routine. Intel had to assure them that the cars belonged to shift workers! Texas Instruments coaches its recruiters to avoid calling students after hours or on weekends so they do not give them the "impression we are here late or routinely working weekends."

Further proof comes in an informal survey of 13 large US employers on the mood around the nation's campuses. Eleven cited changes in questions asked by prospective hires. Students today, the survey noted, do not hesitate to ask questions like, "How long do you typically work in a day?" and "How long do you work in a week?" They noted that recruits now ask, "how do people work together, how are people treated and is the work environment friendly and supportive?"

What top managers in Europe and the USA need to take on board is that the press write-ups of Silicon Valley whiz-kids who never go home and workaholic London financial types is not the norm but the opposite of the way most young workers want to live their lives.

To move, or not to move, that's the question

Another issue that top management must tackle is the mobility issue. And here, I have to say I have some sympathy, because there are mixed signals in the marketplace. While the press writes stories about highly mobile executives who flit through airports with bulging briefcases, schlepping lap-tops and other road-warrior toys, the truth would seem to be more prosaic.

Sure there is a hard-core that like to move all the time, fitting in meetings around Europe or across the Atlantic. But the truth is that it is a very small percentage. Additionally, the ones who have done it know that delayed flights, lost luggage and lousy hotel service are the reality. Those adverts of executive-raincoat-man dashing through a curiously uncrowded airport concourse with a smile on his face are just that, advertising. Possibly the two nastiest places on earth around seven o'clock at night on any Friday are Chicago's O'Hare and London's Heathrow airports.

Thousands of tired, travel-soiled executives in rumpled suits (who says Friday is dress-down?) spill off moving walkways and trample on anyone or anything in their path in their Lemming-like rush to the suburbs. This is the reality, organization man in the raw, having just emerged from a packed plane, where even in business class he has fought for elbow-room, squashed into a middle seat.

Again, that doesn't tell the whole story. What would seem to be the truth, is that our young, eager graduates are quite willing to travel – until they find out what it is really like. This gets translated into the daft idea that everyone wants a job abroad.

Here are two views: A survey by the Community of European Management Schools notes that for 73 percent of graduates, "job mobility is not only desirable but strongly requested." Companies with offices abroad are viewed positively. According to the study, "graduates want an employer that not only offers opportunities for personal development (95%) but one that is innovative (92.5%)." Pay, they reported, ranked third.

A MORI poll for search firm TMP polled 104 chief executives, where 56 percent said they were just sick and tired of jumping on and off planes and it was time someone else did it. The reason TMP commissioned the study was to discover the unwillingness of some top managers to relocate from one country to another.

Here we must also make something clear. In talent mobility we have to consider two things:

- relocation to a new location in possibly another country on an assignment on semi-permanent basis;
- Constant travel, week-after-week.

Depending on who you are and your lifestyle plans, you may – or may not – want to try it out. But the message that this should send to managers everywhere is:

- don't assume people want to travel, just because some magazine article says they do;

- check carefully, what your current *cadre* of managers really thinks of the lifestyle you have imposed on them;

- realize that you may have to re-define the image you are creating in the market. What you might need to do is make it clear that travel is an option, if you want it, but isn't an absolute necessity to succeed. For every hot young talent who dreams of foreign horizons, there's a mediocre one just itching to stay home!

FILL THOSE SHOES!

Leopard-skin stilettos, sequinned dancing shoes and hiking boots fronted a recruitment campaign by bankers UBS Warburg. Under the slogan, "get those shoes filled" the investment banker offered employees from £3,000 to £5,000 to help them hire new recruits. Warburg told employees, "this rewards you for helping to bring the right people to your organization – people who fit." They added, "It'll make your social life easier to plan too."

Maybe UBS Warburg are thinking too traditionally. In internet advertising company DoubleClick there were two Harley-Davidson motorbikes decorating the reception area. They were prizes for the employees who introduced the highest number of new recruits to the company.

More fuel for the fire

If all of us haven't quite accepted the modern work-world reality, let's look at another study, *Riding the Wave: the New Global Career Structure* published by The Career Innovation Research Group. They took 1,000 young professionals from all over the world and asked them what they wanted in a job, a career, and – I guess – life. They highlighted nine key findings. Let's look at these in the context of what these high-potential-flyers want, and how your firm could become a talent magnet for them.

Today's young international high-flyers have a short career horizon and it will be difficult – but not impossible – for companies to retain them.

This is certainly true, and firms must "get this" once and for all. Don't be surprised when people leave, just know how and where to get more.

At the bottom of the list of "career values" is stability. Instead, high-flyers reply more on their employability – their ability to keep their options open and maximize their personal and professional development – to ensure future success.

Not too sure about this – it could be just the age-group speaking. My view is that as they age the urge to move lessens. The secret is knowing when you can make an offer that will keep them for a long time: and knowing what the offer needs to be.

Achieving work/life balance is one of the greatest challenges these people face. Almost all (94%) are willing to work long hours to some extent, but nearly one-fifth of these men and women would like to work part-time and 41 percent would like more choice over working hours.

Oh yes. Work 10 days straight, fine, but then let me take four days off to party. Can't offer me that and I'm outta here.

Despite their short-term career intention, young professionals still express loyalty to their managers. However, the greatest commitment is to their immediate colleagues and staff. This highlights the negative effects when an individual is dissatisfied and leaves.

Our inability as managers to reach out and engage these people is a disgrace. Why can't we be better at it? One leaves and the others sense trouble like animals at a waterhole. They don't know why they get jumpy to move, they just do.

The majority of these future leaders have a strong psychological "performance contract" with their employers, but most are searching for a "development contract." Almost half report that their company only invests in their personal development "to a little extent" (39%) or "not at all" (10%).

More to be ashamed about. These people want to develop – if we cannot offer them that, someone else will.

Over two-thirds (69%) say that an international work assignment is important for their personal development. Thirty-six percent would be willing to live and work abroad for more than five years and, surprisingly, almost half of those with a partner (48%), or with children (46%) report that their mobility is not constrained.

I can relate to this, what gets them (as I already mentioned) is the constant travel. Of course they'll move while they can, but they want a place to call "home" wherever that is.

Their top three career values are: wide horizons; work/life balance and professional expertise. Wide horizons refers to maximizing future options, meeting new people and having new and different experiences.

These are networkers, and they stay in touch with people. That's why they know what's fun and where. Because they do this automatically they are practically fireproof, they'll never be lost for a "next logical step" to take.

Just as they seek development for themselves, 85 percent are also willing to coach and develop junior colleagues. However, less than half say that their employer expects this, reinforcing for the next generation the belief that development is not a corporate priority.

This is bad news. They have a lot to give and a lot of knowledge to pass on. Help them do that.

Despite an apparent reluctance to take risks, many list start-up companies among their alternative career options. Other preferences include working for voluntary agencies, non-government organizations and – especially – the UN.

Said this earlier. People have choices brought about by more independence and a different view on life. Learn that they aren't bound by your views of a career... it just isn't the same for these people. Learn the new reality – really quick.

It's not just the travel – It's Relocation... period

There have always been business people eager to relocate to another city or country and certainly that is still the case. However, it is getting harder for many companies to get people to come and work for them. One of the key reasons is that for the majority these days, both partners in a relationship or marriage tend to work.

Even executives who years ago signed an agreement with their firm that they were mobile now demur when it comes to actually doing it. Everyone from top managers to newly married junior executives look very closely at the suggestion. Usually it is because the spouse has a job that they are not willing to leave, but it can be other factors like children reaching a critical moment in school, ageing parents or even the fact that they have a great life – outside of work – where they are currently living. Other issues that impact are a lack of opportunity for the spouse at the new location (often work permits can be a hassle), no decent, or inferior, schooling for children.

Today, a lot of managers would rather do the commute Monday to Friday than uproot the whole family. Where once there was no question about relocating, now there are other options. These are options that companies seeking to recruit needed talent are going to have to embrace. And in this complex business world there are three cases that illustrate that it isn't just a question of making an offer. All sorts of thinking about lifestyle goes into the decision-making process. We need to better understand what is motivating people to work and that this can quickly change. Each of these cases is real, just the locations have changed. All occurred in 2001.

A senior engineer (53) gets offered a general management position at group headquarters. He lives in Stockholm, HQ is in Frankfurt. His wife is a doctor in a local hospital, they have three children all in school. Both have ageing parents. He is also captain of his local golf club. After some thought he takes the job because he realizes that he travels so much anyway that he doesn't have to uproot the family. He commutes to Frankfurt a few days a week (on average) but in reality, with a global responsibility, he is usually on a plane somewhere anyway on a Monday. He insists on a small flat near his German office and extracts a written undertaking that he gets to be home on Friday nights (unless he is around the other side of the globe) and has his weekends with his family. That's the way organizations have to think if they want to hire talent. They need to realize that there has been a great deal of change in what executives will or will not do.

A 43 year-old organizational development manager for a major multinational is based outside London, 50 miles from Heathrow Airport. As part of his job he travels to the firm's HQ in a Chicago suburb for meetings – which lately have increased dramatically. He finds that in six months he has crossed the Atlantic nine times. Usually, this means leaving on a Sunday afternoon and getting back on a Saturday morning. He is married with two young children and his wife is not at all amused at being left for so many nights and having weekends ruined. One night the phone rings and the head-hunter calls with a lucrative offer. Good position, good money and central London-based. Two interviews later, he is offered the job, then the thinking begins. What he has discovered about the prospective job is that the company has a long hours culture. He works out that he will have to get up at six every morning, to catch a train to get him into the office by eight-thirty. On the reverse commute, it is unlikely he will be able to leave before six-thirty, which means with travel time he can't be home before the children go to bed. Also there is the prospect of staying up in London overnight for late meetings and entertaining customers at least once each week and stories of weekend "planning" retreats. When he closely examines this against his current trans-Atlantic work life, he realizes that his current job is better. Certainly he often leaves on a Sunday, but he has a car to take him to Heathrow. He has an automatic upgrade to first class and a limousine to pick him up at the other end. Two or three times he takes his wife along to Chicago. When he is in the UK he can take days to work from home with no complaint. He stayed with his employer.

A Dutch marketing executive, 46 has a secret ambition, that few of his closet friends really know. He wants to live in the South of France. To this end, he and his wife buy a property and over several years convert it to suit their purposes. Their idea is that someday, when they are ready to retire, they will live there full time. One day in January his wife loses her job. He is not too happy about his – it entails a great deal of short travel, going to London, Paris, Zurich for the day. He hears of a job open in Paris that fits his profile. He is interviewed and takes it. They rent a small apartment in Paris (the children are all out of the house pursuing their own lives). Then the new high-speed link between Paris and the south opens. They can get to their dream house in less than three hours by train and a 30 minute drive. What does he do – commute, of course. He does a deal in a local one star hotel to have a permanent room. He leaves Paris every Friday afternoon (or often heads back from a trip somewhere in Europe) at four or five in the evening and is home for late dinner. On Monday morning he gets up early and takes the first train to Paris. If ever there was a happy commuter this is it. We should realize that this is going to increase as more and more people realize the options fast-rail links provide.

What these three cases show, is that if we want talent and if we want to retain it, we can't think in those old ways anymore. People weigh up options in ways they would never have considered a decade ago. To be a talent magnet we have to put on a very different face and be prepared to deal with expectations and demands that are only just being realized.

THEY LOOKED SO GOOD, WE BOUGHT THE COMPANY

UK telecommunications components maker Filtronic launched an innovative take-over of US-based Sigtek, in which the amount they pay will depend on how many of the engineers stay for more than four years. "The business isn't that interesting for us," said Filtronic, " what we want are the people and this is easier than trying to recruit 23 engineers one-by-one."

Location, location, location

Here we are back with Conrad Hilton's favorite phrase, location, location, location. But if it's all about people with options and a new lifestyle in their minds, then the location issue goes firmly hand-in-hand with that. New ways of living and the desire to live in the best places are prompting people to move. It is shaping the search for talent too. Three things seem to dominate:

- There are havens of talent, that if you want to hire you need to be part of. Equally, there are places – that given today's choice – no-one except the desperate or possibly criminal would be seen dead in.

- There are an increasing number of people who are making choices about where they want to live, because it suits their lifestyle, like those I described above. This is going to increase.

- Technology has changed the equation too. You can live up a Swiss alp and do business as long as you are prepared to come down from time to time and meet people.

When I suggested earlier that people didn't want to move that much, what I should have said was they didn't want to be forced to move for a job. They want to be in control and they want the option of saying "no" if it doesn't meet their criteria.

What we have seen in the past few years is the rise of certain locations as preferred places of work. Places where employees can easily establish themselves and create a work/life balance that meets current criteria for a whole variety of reasons.

In Europe, hot cities are drawing hot talent, creating a real renaissance that often gets overlooked. For example, a gentle curve on a map from Barcelona, across southern France, northern Italy, Switzerland and southern Germany, already boast the highest per capita income level in the world. What companies are quickly discovering is that if they don't move to where the talent is swarming like worker bees they are going to have great difficulty in getting the people they need.

In Europe, consider these locations as turn-ons that bear a close scrutiny.

Amsterdam

The Dutch capital has a reputation as a liberal city, which suits the lifestyle of the creative types who flock here in search of opportunity. Philips moved here from dowdy, un-trendy Eindhoven to boost its ability to recruit foreign talent.

Brussels

It might be labeled a boring burg, but Brussels is a small, livable city and being home to the European Union, NATO and over 1,000 foreign multinationals boasts great schools, good infrastructure, highly affordable housing and a highly educated, multi-lingual local workforce. US corporations still regard this as the "safe option" when they go into Europe. Just beware swingeing local taxes on income and make sure you are clearly classed as an expatriate.

London

Huge and dirty, with a transport system that creaks to a halt frequently and sky high property prices and school fees, many wonder at London's continued success as a talent magnet. There are many: the key being its very hugeness and the fact that the natives speak English – the world's business *lingua franca*. London is the most cosmopolitan city on the planet, with more non-Brits living in it than any other metropolis. Despite what Frankfurt and Paris have tried, it is still, with New York, the center of the world's banking industry. Today, entertainment, advertising and new media, make it a Mecca for all kind of talent. And it is, of course, the European home to more US multinationals than anywhere else. Companies keep moving in because it is so international. Add to that the fact that the area 50 miles around Heathrow is home to many other international headquarters and you have one of the largest infrastructures in the world – shame about the trains though!

Zurich

Once dubbed the "most boring city in Europe", Zurich has changed. With the lake on its front doorstep, so clean that secretaries go swimming at lunch-breaks in the summer and the skiing is visible from your office window, this is the place for those with an active lifestyle. Banks and pharmaceutical companies abound and the Swiss are getting more relaxed about work permits for foreigners. Also, all the young professionals speak English, and most French too. One enterprising Swiss bank, needing e-business talent actually flew in 20 hopefuls from Silicon Valley. They didn't show them the offices, just took them skiing for the weekend and then drove them down to the Mediterranean. No matter their workplace wasn't air-conditioned, 16 signed up for the two-year contract. Now that's thinking about how to be a talent magnet to a tough-to-get them-out-of-their state group.

Nice

It isn't just home to movie stars. Nice and its surroundings are going very high-tech. The Sofia-Antipolis research park is home to some of Europe's major corporations and the atmosphere is cosmopolitan in the extreme. It is estimated that from Monte-Carlo to Barcelona, more than two million foreigners live along the Mediterranean. Many of the companies have summer hours, so you can be on your yacht or in the mountains by mid-afternoon and there's a lot of – still – affordable property and good connections to the outside world.

Berlin

Germany's born-again capital city is home to a high-tech renaissance and a whole lot more, but it is not as international as Frankfurt or Munich, which challenges Zurich in lifestyle and international outlook.

Milan

This is also a hot spot for high-technology as well as the designer houses with a lot of young talent emigrating to its elegant avenues.

Ireland

It's capital Dublin has performed an economic miracle with clever tax-incentives to entice foreign banks and call centers. They are still trying to entice the Irish *diaspora* to come home as they have run out of people.

This is definitely a young city, but through historical connections, very popular with US multinationals, who have an abiding affection for all things Irish.

And a couple of places to watch:

Barcelona
This is setting itself up to be another talent trap. Lifestyle is good and – compared to other parts of Europe – relatively inexpensive. Lots of local talent that speaks good English and French and wants challenge and excitement.

Marbella
This is more than German retirees and resting bank robbers these days. A vibrant young international set are creating new companies and beginning to put it on the map as more than an up market vacation spot. The local mayor sees it as a European Florida. Air connections are improving all the time.

Marseilles
Now less than two hours from Paris, the region around the major port could be set for a new future. However, its Frenchness may hold it back.

Antwerp
This is Europe's second seaport after Rotterdam, but is very international in its outlook and is a creative center as well as home to hundreds of high-tech companies. It's a lot more fun to live there than Brussels (20 miles or so away) and property prices are some of the lowest in Europe. The natives are friendly and all the business executives are quadri-lingual. Again, make sure your personal tax situation is A-OK.

Beware of some others, that on the surface, may be appealing.

Paris
The city of light, doesn't just draw American tourists, it draws eager executives too. But, Paris is one thing: French. Unlike London it isn't a cos-

mopolitan city and it doesn't have a lot of talent that is very international. You need to speak French to really survive. Companies I know have suffered in Paris and they have problems getting people to go to work there. To be frank you are better off in *Lyon* where the software industry and others are located and have enticed a lot of foreign talent and French with international views and vision.

Stockholm

A lot of smart companies are operating in Sweden's capital, but it has two huge drawbacks, taxes and climate: the taxes are high and the climate's cold for much of the time. Oh, and it's a long flight (three hours) to most other European cities). In fact, major Swedish corporations like Ericsson and Securitas have already moved many of their HQ operations to London to be able to attract talent. Good points are that everyone speaks English and education and health care are tops.

Helsinki

The Finnish capital has similar problems to Stockholm, except that its even colder and further to travel. However, companies like Nokia have made themselves a talent magnet by not chasing the obvious. They have search teams in countries like India, where offering good salaries, social benefits and four and five week vacations acts as a great magnet. Upshot is that Helsinki now boasts some of the finest Indian restaurants in Europe.

Others move even further in the search for the right talent. Dutch electronic giant Philips may have moved 50 miles from Eindhoven to Amsterdam for its world headquarters, but it has two divisions located in San Jose, California just to get the talent it needs to do the job. This is the kind of thing that is happening all over, as firms look to see where is the best place to be for the future.

In the USA things are changing too. While New York is an ongoing magnet for international talent, other cities are fighting to get their share by creating quality-of-place as a lifestyle choice. Richard Florida, a location specialist, carried out a study of what's happening in the USA for the Carnegie Mellon University. Here's his view.

"The rise of the new economy has radically altered the ways that cities and regions [in the USA] establish and maintain their competitive advantage. In the new economy, regions develop an advantage based on their ability to quickly mobilize the best people, resources and capabilities required to turn innovations into new business ideas and commercial products. The nexus of competitive advantage has thus shifted to those regions that can generate, attract and retain the best talent."

Richard Florida's study highlights six key factors in the location war. They apply just as much to Europe and parts of Asia as the USA. They are an excellent summary of what the new-economy worker expects and is determined to get. If we want these people to work for us, we need to be able to meet their needs one way or another.

Quality-of-place
Natural, recreational and lifestyle amenities are absolutely vital in attracting knowledge workers and in supporting leading-edge high-technology firms. Knowledge workers essentially balance economic opportunity and lifestyle in selecting a place to live and work. Thus, quality-of-place factors are as important as traditional economic factors such as jobs and career opportunity in attracting knowledge workers. Given that they have a wealth of job opportunities, knowledge workers have the ability to choose cities and regions that are attractive places to live as well as work.

Availability of jobs
Plenty of job and career opportunities is a necessary – but insufficient – condition to attract knowledge workers. Knowledge workers favor cities and regions with a "thick labor market" which offers the wide variety of employment opportunities required to sustain a career. Quality-of-place completes the picture.

Amenities and environment
Leading regions also rate very highly in terms of quality-of-place with

high levels of amenities and environmental quality. Austin, Texas, Seattle, Washington, the San Francisco Bay area, the greater Boston region, and Washington DC score consistently high across virtually every quality-of-place measure. There is a strikingly strong correlation across the board between regions that are home to a large concentration of knowledge workers, amenities and the environment.

Aggressive activity

Leading regions have aggressively pursued strategies to bolster their environmental quality, natural amenities and lifestyle offerings to attract and retain talent. Austin and Seattle have placed a high priority on recreational amenities such as bike paths, mountain bike trails, parks, recreational areas and accessibility to water for rowing and sailing. These regions have cultivated thriving music scenes and are also known for their youth oriented cultures that are open and supportive of diversity. Both regions are among the national leaders in smart growth and sustainable development.

Diversity rules

New-economy workers prefer places with a diverse range of outdoor recreational activities and associated lifestyle amenities. They prefer regions where amenities are easy to get at and available on a "just-in-time" basis. Due to long hours, fast pace and tight deadlines associated with much knowledge work they require amenities that blend seamlessly with work and can be accessed on demand. They favor cities and regions that offer a wide range of experiences which are youth oriented and supportive of demographic diversity.

As we move further into the 21st century it becomes pretty clear that any company that wants talent is going to have to consider how it is going to get it. If we continue to stress that most jobs are short term – and that we are no longer offering 30 or even 20 year careers then we have to expect that a lot of talent will huddle protectively together for collective warmth. What talent wants is to be fairly certain that when one job hits a dead end there is another around the corner. While I totally agree with Richard Florida's observations, there is one slight flaw. If you tire of your job in a city like Seattle, it is one hell of a long way to go for job interviews – south of San Francisco or east to Boston and New York. Europeans are luckier, distances are shorter, but this still (as I already suggested) means that cities on the periphery (Stockholm, Oslo, Helsinki, Athens, Istanbul, Madrid, Rome) will have to fight that much harder to not only attract talent but keep what its already got. Having said that, others will go for a gentler lifestyle, hoping that the company they opt to work for in bucolic surroundings in a Swiss, Spanish or Welsh valley, or will stay successful and they won't have to try and job search too soon.

I have a client with a factory unit on the Atlantic coast of France. The first thing they ask you when you arrive at reception after the obligatory *bonjour* is, "how many oysters would you like for lunch because we are just sending down to the fish dock for them." You feel you could get to like working in an atmosphere like that!

Of course, talent has always migrated to cities and always will. What we are now seeing is the importance of a region, which does offer a lot more options as networking and following the activities of competitors becomes that much easier.

DRESS UP THERE!

Office supplies group OfficeSMART says its survey of workers shows that dress-down days have lost their popularity. Men, in particular prefer their suits and ties and most stick to office dress codes. Of those who don't over a third said that they actually dressed more smartly than required and two-thirds say that smart dressing commands respect. Around one in three think that dress-down days give rise to a holiday atmosphere in the office.

And then think workplace ...

If talent migrates to what it perceives are cool cities that offer cutting-edge opportunity, then they will also migrate to offices that mirror the lifestyle they are seeking. Lately, new offices are reflecting these expectations by giving people a lot more than a cubicle, a pot plant and a PC. Offices with atriums, offices with espresso and sushi bars, offices with gyms and pools in the basement. This is a trend designed to get the attention of people who want to work, but expect more than average surroundings. Certainly, if a candidate has two offers and one is in some old-style office block and the other is in a new-style work-environment with all the toys added in for good measure, it is going to be no contest which position they take.

Even the venerable old-style companies are taking this seriously. Ford has created a Richard Rogers-designed office for their global design staff right in the heart of London's Soho. The idea is that the designers from all over the globe will come together and work (and possibly play too) in the midst of a highly creative environment. The building includes a trendy noodle bar and other delights to help the designers think creative new thoughts.

The Los Angeles offices of advertising agency TBWA/Chiat Day are even cooler than that, they have been designed like an urban neighborhood. Informally known as Advertising City, the floor is bisected by a central corridor called Main Street, and in the centre is a café and a stand of trees called Central Park. In addition there's a basketball court, a games room and a bar. According to the designers employees are in "snug workstations, called nests and the nests are grouped together in areas that radiate out from Main Street like Parisian *arrondissements*."

In a business park outside London, not far from Windsor Castle a developer has created another new-age style office concept. Here employees of the fifteen or so different firms who rent space there, can plug in laptops outside in the grounds on sunny days, or use the open plan restaurant and work-out areas. At British Airways' headquarters not far away, employees can stroll beside an indoor river.

Even the French are not being outdone in the change of expectation for what a workplace should be. Alstom Transport's headquarters building outside Paris, is an all-glass atrium, with an espresso bar on the ground floor, where you can get warm croissants every morning and read the world's newspapers. At nine o'clock it is the epicenter of the firm, with people talking to each other about business or last night's soccer game. Above their heads, are seating areas overlooking the atrium with comfortable sofas and drinking fountains. In the basement there is a state-of-the-art gym.

Trendy? Maybe. Does it matter? If you want to capture hearts and minds of talent this is what it is going to take. If all you've got to offer is a machine that purveys soggy sandwiches and plastic coffee, you'd better take note.

And let's remember that all of this is about engaging the employees. At the end of the day what it does is get employees out of their offices and meeting each other instead of e-mailing. It gets talent talking.

My favorite story about this is in a distinctly un-trendy Madison Avenue, New York advertising agency. I am sitting in a reception waiting to see the chairman, when the elevator doors open and out shoots an electric golf-cart all togged up like a pizza truck. With bells ringing and lights flashing, it shot off down a corridor.

"What was THAT!" I asked the receptionist?

"That was the chairman," she replied, "he does it a couple of times a week. Gives out free pizza around the building." Later, pizza slice in hand, I asked him what it was all about.

"I realized," he said, "that people were sitting in cubicles communicating electronically through partitions. No-one was talking. We are in the creative business, we need to share ideas, not just in meetings, but informally. I thought, this'll get them into the corridors – and boy, oh boy, it does!"

Not just the place to hang your hat though

There's a danger here in talking too much about cool places that attract talent and hot-shot offices that cement it into place. We also have to consider the type of job we are asking the talent to do. If we can get that right, where headquarters is doesn't always matter. Here's a case that illustrates what I mean.

Recently, on a Friday night, I was flying from Paris to Southampton, my local regional airport in southern England. The Friday night flight is always full and I am squeezed into my tiny seat (French people are a different shape from me!) next to a young woman. We get talking. She is going home for the weekend to her parents who live in the New Forest in Hampshire, where she was brought up. I ask her who she works for, she explains that she started a few months ago with a large insurance firm that is based in Bradford in Yorkshire. Bradford, is not Monte-Carlo, Bradford (with apologies to the city fathers isn't even Pittsburgh, it's a run down city in England's northern rust belt). "That must be a bit of a difference," I suggest, "it's not exactly the New Forest, more the concrete jungle." She agrees. So, why does she work there? "I don't," is the reply, "I work in Budapest." And, as we bounce across the English Channel she explains that she was a language student, had spent two years in Spain, and was hoping to eventually work out there for this company. In the meantime she was helping out on the firm's Hungarian launch. She was ecstatically happy, doing a challenging, exciting job. So before we assume that all the talent is in the trendy towns in smooth offices, let's consider what we want our talent to do – and where.

Another view is held by Grey Advertising who bought a small e-advertising business, Beyond Interactive in Ann Arbor, Michigan. Grey used the company they bought to train-up new talent from an abundant local supply. Grey says that at Beyond Interactive it hires for attitude and trains for skills. That way they get 60 new employees each month who are willing to try new things and are eager to improve. And the choice of a university town with rich talent but few other employment opportunities was inspirational.

There is, of course, a downside. These people will get good and get restless and move on. Knowing when talent is ready to fly from the nest is something we need to spend more time thinking about as well.

NEW FACES IN AN OLD SHELL

Royal Dutch/Shell has long recruited its managers from the universities of the UK and the Netherlands and its top management *cadre* reflects this – no longer. Under a "new broom" initiative by their head of HR, John Hofmeister (an ex-Allied Signal American), they have set themselves the goal of having 10–15 percent of its senior management recruited from outside the group. Proving that even the most massive, set-in-their-ways conservative organizations can change when it comes to being a talent magnet.

Let loose the talent trackers

It seems to me that the world has changed fast and a lot of us haven't noticed. Maybe we've been too busy making money, making products, fighting off acquisitions, buying up others. But that's what CEOs and other senior managers do. What is needed now, if we are to get serious about being a talent magnet is to get some people working on this – full time.

Imagine just how much you could save in lost business (people take it with them), lost time (the frustration of interviews) and lost money (new people always cost more than those who quit), if you had one person or a team of people looking for talent and making sure that once you've got it, it stays.

We can say blandly that it is everyone's job to hire and hold talent. That may be true, in theory, but little else. We all get busy, we will get focussed on what, ultimately pays our salary and secures our future. Many of us don't have time for anything else. Management can come up with ideas like "refer a friend and win big money", but it still leaves a lot missing.

If there really is a shortage of talent – and it is going to get a whole lot worse – and we really need to be a magnet for it, then we need to do this in a professional way. We need someone who lights the talent beacon and keeps the flame alive. We need someone who can cross boundaries and departments to helping others to achieve better talent recruitment, recognition and retention.

They have been trying out something like this in some Wall Street and City of London banks. Most managers in banks don't like people: they are high-performing specialists, who might encourage their team, but little else. Realizing that people management – and poor people management at that – just gets in the way of these experts making money, banks have begun to assign professional people managers to the manager's group. These "professional people persons" do the "soft" stuff, wipe noses, motivate, fill in the forms, do the feedback sessions and in general provide a superior executive nanny service.

Maybe this is one of the things we need to consider in other industries. Have talent managers that allow the experts to get on with what they do best. If the only talent they'll worry about is those immediately around them who can make business and make money for the firm, then it is high time we took the people concerns (if they are concerned at all) away from them.

Talent managers – some companies already have them. You should too.

Can you make a difference?

This book is about how companies can become magnets for talent. It is also about suggesting ways that individual managers – not CEOs or HR supremos – can make their own part of the business a talent magnet. What is it that a team leader or business unit manager can do? What can be put in place easily if it looks as though headquarters aren't going to do too much about this talent magnet thing? Hopefully, if this is your current situation, you'll pick up ideas throughout the book that can be implemented by you personally. What I am going to do here, is give a quick summary of actions you can take yourself. On page x of the book, is an e-mail address where you can send any GREAT ideas you have (GREAT ideas only please!). They would all be welcome.

Individual action

Worried that your current employer isn't taking being a magnet for talent seriously? Well if it really concerns you, there is one easy option – LEAVE! Now that is taking direct action, which may get them to take notice! If this doesn't appear to be an option, think about things this way: what are the actions that you can take to source and secure the people you need?

As I have described earlier, people and places dominate this war for talent. Assuming you have a reasonable amount of freedom to do things your way, consider:

- what kind of people do you need to achieve your goals?
- can you source them where you are located?
- do you have difficulty getting them to want to join you?
- if so, why?

Then, can you:

- change your location? Not necessarily by a major move, but just to a more convenient location for the people you want to hire (e.g. closer to transport links, closer to an airport, in a city location)
- look in other places for people who would find the job and the place attractive? (e.g. as Nokia did by looking to hire out-of-Europe talent)
- change the office location or refit it to meet the needs of the talent you require?
- give them additional perks like laptops, opportunities to work at home, memberships of gyms and to cultural events?

Oh, and pets too!

California company Software City is a pet-lovers paradise. More than 100 of the employees bring their dogs, cats and rabbits to work each day. Sounds crazy, but the employees (and they say the pets too) love it.

While this may sound a wacky way to run a business, consider this. Like-minded people cluster together. What this firm has found is one of the secrets. People who like animals like being together and that includes during work time. Maybe it is going too far for most, but we need to think of these types of initiatives if we want to attract the talent we need.

Then again if the CFO is allergic to fur...

LIFE 101

Not only do companies have to train workers today for entry-level positions, they have to help them cope with life in general. At Burger King, basic training for starting restaurant jobs now includes what they term "Life 101". This includes items like teaching new employees how to balance a checkbook, and getting to work on time.

4 Lighting your own talent beacon

You can fool all of the people all of the time.
If the advertising is right and the budget is
big enough.

JOSEPH E LEVINE

Too much of a good thing is wonderful.

MAE WEST

Talent in the real world

It's five o'clock on a wet and windy Friday night. Your staff are drifting toward the elevators, heading for a weekend of relaxation after a week of hard work. Everyone's happy except you. Why? One of your top sales-people quit this afternoon. Can't stop him: the offer is too good. Can't hold him back: we should have promoted him months ago. Need help: HR are sympathetic, but busy.

HR are ALWAYS busy. HR actually say that they are the busiest department in any corporation on the planet. No-one knows quite why, but THEY are busy. Whether they are busy doing the right things is, of course, open to question. But, usually that's why you can't get their help when you need it and why (they themselves admit) in this complex busi-ness world, where the stakes in the ongoing battle for talent keep getting higher, they are not giving the support they should. The consequence of this is that more and more line managers find themselves having to take on the responsibility for getting new talent into the business.

A survey by consultants PricewaterhouseCoopers of 900 plus European companies proved the point. HR professionals say that they should be spending their time on:

- Organizational and culture change;
- Leadership development;
- Internal communication.

But actually spend it on:

- payroll;
- administration;
- training and education.

That makes it pretty clear that, for whatever reasons – no matter how good they may be – there are going to be lots and lots of inconvenient, high pressure times when HR will not come through and line managers will just have to do their own thing. In the scrappy atmosphere of today's talent wars that can be practically all the time.

What this means – and we had all better understand it – is that if you are a local manager, or head of a business unit, you will have no other choice than be your own magnet for talent. Most probably, HR will give you back-up in the form of getting contracts signed and ironing out policies and procedures and final offers, but the line manager is going to be put increasingly on the spot.

And why not? It is a business truism that "people join companies, but leave bosses." It is because of the boss they have, that people – ultimately – take the mental decision to stay or go. Therefore, line managers need to either develop the people skills that will make them a magnet for talent or find some people who can help them achieve that.

So many of us today work in remote teams and task forces that we need to find useful ways to not only keep the people assigned to us, but to send out signals that promote us as a talent magnet.

So what can you do?

The first thing to do – and this is backed up by a great number of discussions with managers who are hell bent on creating a talent magnet profile in their part of the business – is make sure just how much leeway you have.

Talk to your boss and get a clear signal about how much freedom you have to:

- keep your team or department happy;
- go the extra mile to hold onto talent you need;
- hire talent that beats a path to your door, by design or accidentally (we'll come back to that later).

Let's look at these in a little more detail.

Freedom to keep your team happy

If your part of the business is doing great, or you are chalking up milestones in a project faster than planned, you need the freedom to reward your team. If your management is serious about having talented individuals work for them this won't be a problem. But people can stand in the way. It will tell you a lot about the company you are working with, just what reaction you get. But go for it! Remember, if it isn't appreciated, other firms hire individuals but they also hire teams!

Freedom to hold onto talent

When talent says it is leaving, how much autonomy do you have to negotiate a package that might change their mind? In this fast-paced business world, when HR specialists and your direct report might be hundreds or thousands of miles away, you don't have time to play around with long negotiations and a host of counter offers. Get a clear – in writing – mandate of how far you can go if the going gets tough. All the signs are that managers are going to find themselves more on their own than ever, so make sure you have the right ammunition and know how to set it off.

Freedom to hire talent

Just how flexible is your organization? Don't wait until it's too late to test it out – find out. If someone asks for a job and you think they'll be great, can you hire them? Go and ask the classic question that I developed years ago for a client.

You are sitting sipping a cool drink at 35,000 feet, thinking about nothing in particular and you get talking to the guy/gal in the seat next to yours. You quickly realize that this person is the one person that can make a major change to your part of the business. The question is, can you offer them a job? Or is the bureaucratic process so pervasive, that the best you could say was, "Hey, I'll get back to you." In this war for talent, if you see the person you know can most help out – you must be able to hire them. If you can't, you'll never be a beacon for talent and they'll know it.

Many, many smart executives who I have known over the years – a lot of them now in senior positions in major corporations – say that if you meet someone who's very, very good, you'll know in about 30 seconds flat. All of them also offer the same piece of advice: "Hire them on the spot, or you'll never see them again."

But why should that be the prerogative of the CEO and his merry band of followers. It's the line guys doing the work and they know what they want. And when you realize that in today's working world – a world governed by the churn of executives from one job to another – over 40 percent of all new hires leave within 12 months, what's the big deal if they didn't turn out to be as good as you thought, anyway. Hell you saved a head-hunters fee, didn't you?

Simple strategies for having and holding

It doesn't really matter whether we are a lowly line manager or the chief executive – everything is relative. This list below makes a good start in taking on the personal responsibility of being a talent magnet: finding and fixing your team.

Hang out where the talent hangs out

Maybe we just got too sophisticated and forgot how to do things ourselves. Jim or Jill quit and we pick up the phone, call the recruiters or the head-hunters and then wait. I don't think we have the luxury to wait. Almost daily I hear the moans and groans of managers who say that search firms are too slow. To that the search firms respond that their clients are too impatient and don't understand the marketplace: "the guy wants Einstein tomorrow morning, but he doesn't want to pay," is the complaining refrain.

Thirty years ago, when there weren't many professional recruiters, managers knew where the talent was – now they need to learn that again. I often use in presentations the story of the Portuguese manager who, faced with a huge new piece of business, knew exactly who he wanted for the job. "I just went to where he had lunch everyday and booked the table next to his," was the remark. How simple. Why can't we learn to do that? Possibly because most of us have forgotten how to have lunch. Can you meet talent in a sandwich queue? Possibly. Can you meet it in the executive dining room? Doubtful. Maybe we need to start and broaden our horizons again. If we want to meet talent let's find out where it is and go meet it – live and in the flesh. Oh, and let's start having lunch too!

Know who you want and why

First rule. Don't fill the job, hire the person who can make a contribution. Too many of us see the hole in the organization chart as a challenge to be solved. Not true. Appraise that job. Is it what's necessary or should it be something else? Also, be sure of the kind of person you need and what you want them to do. Chances are that a half-hour's reflection will give you a whole new view on what you want and the way you want the job to work out.

Bring in people who bring ideas

You don't want someone who will just "do the job". You need someone who is going to make a difference, look at it in a different way, take the status quo and challenge it. If we are going to be a talent magnet, we need to be a place where new ideas and freedom to think differently flourish.

Think of wacky recruitment ploys

Hiring talent doesn't have to be a hum-drum affair. Think of new ways to reach the people you want. Why just use recruiters or search firms? Go to conferences where the people you want to hire will be, join professional groups. Create a buzz in articles in business publications that will arouse interest. If you are looking for college recruits, by-pass the standard interview ploys and find out where they hang-out. Run website competitions, offer them internships (in foreign subsidiaries goes down a treat). Create focus groups that help locals see what your business is all about. Think what would have got your interest when you were their age (better still, ask your kids). A friend of mine had his two boys do a summer internship at his firm – a large food major. They went reluctantly. Later they explained, "Once we got in there it was great, but the image your firm gives out is so boring that we really dreaded it." That's true of a lot of big corporations. How can you seek to change that in the part that you run?

When you find it hire it fast

Another complaint I get all the time from search firms is, "we found the candidates, but we can't get the manager to call them." Strangely, managers – and the more senior the worse they are – seem to have problems calling candidates to talk. A psychologist friend of mine says that they don't want to appear to be "begging a candidate or selling a job." I think it is an ego thing. "I'll keep them waiting and they'll see how important I am." Well, you can be important, but most likely you'll lose the candidate. Today, no-one is going to hang around and wait. If your office is in New York and the candidate is in London and you happen to be in Hong Kong for a week, for goodness sake fly them out to meet you. We don't have time for this jockeying for position anymore. If your people do it – fire them!

Get to know them

Another complaint that comes up frequently is, "I was hired, started the job and they forgot about me." Don't let that happen. Get to know people so that they not only feel at home, but feel you care about their future. Also you need to know just how good they are and what they might want to do in the future. Spend time with them, nurture them, it will pay you back handsomely. Another thing that is useful – although most of us are shy of prying – is to get to know something of their private lives, often a hard job to do in places like Europe). Knowing their personal circumstances can help to better decision making or being prepared. Are they married? Will they start a family. Does the spouse work and does that limit mobility? These are all questions better answered if you know something about their personal plans.

Don't forget the people you inherited

Many of us fail at the first hurdle. We inherit a team or department and are so busy getting the people we want on board we never look at what we've been given. I firmly believe that huge amounts of talent lie buried in organizations and we totally underutilize it. We don't find it and people never tell you, because you didn't ask. This has to be one of the greatest forms of waste in our corporations today. So, find out what you've got in your department and find out what their aspirations really are.

Find out who they know

Again, I think that everyone has hidden talents and we just don't use them. Hire a new employee for the skills you expect, but find out what else they can do. Often people spend a working lifetime in the wrong job. We can expand our talent base just by looking at what we have and making an audit of their skills.

Empower your people/give responsibility

Peak performers today expect freedom to act – give it to them, as much as they want. We cannot stifle talent or ring-fence it. If we do it will leave.

Younger talent especially wants to be given opportunities to succeed and to fail and we have to make sure that the climate we foster allows that. If you are scared about it don't be. Just spend a lot of time with them so you can maintain a discreet watching brief over what is happening. And when things work out, don't wait until they get a rival offer from another firm (and they will if they are any good), move them up quickly even if it means losing them from your area of influence (you'll have made a friend for life and a future committed colleague).

Not all talent expects promotion

It is also useful to remember that a lot of talent doesn't want to be a top manager, even if it got the chance. Talent comes in all shapes, sizes and ambitions and it is up to the smart manager to recognize that. Personally, I think too much emphasis is still placed on being upwardly mobile. A lot of the talent that we need is specialist and should probably never have people responsibilities (likewise, a lot of it should never be let out to meet customers or shareholders either!). If you do your homework right, you'll know who wants to do what, and hopefully why they can't always achieve those ambitions. Learn to deal with non-promotability.

Mentor them

If they are young, find them a mentor who can help them grow. Chances are high they'll both appreciate it and it can build remarkably productive relationships. At the same time it sends out good vibes all round. The younger employees see you mean what you say about letting them grow, the older ones see you appreciate their skills and knowledge.

Reward them

I'm not just talking money and other perks. If they do a great job find ways to give them surprise rewards: a weekend's vacation, a trip that they can take their wife along. Don't bury these, let the rest of your people know why and treat everyone the same, IF they perform. Make sure that your manager knows about what you do and if they don't approve, fight for it tooth and nail. I know managers who have been refused these sorts of reward strategies by their bosses and have just done it out of their own pocket to keep the relationship on a high.

Communicate

There is, to my mind, nothing more important than clear, ongoing communication between a manager and the people who work for him or her. Don't wait for the headquarters to do it, do it yourself. As so many of us have employees scattered in many locations, travelling or working on customer sites, good, open communication is paramount. And not just by e-mail or phone either. Get them together, share ideas, experiences and concerns. Be open with them and they'll be open with you. A failure to communicate, to let people know what's happening, destroys talent, and it doesn't take very long. As most of us work in organizations where we have knowledge workers, we need to treat them with respect. Don't let them find out for themselves (which they will anyway) tell them what's happening and why.

Don't oversell

You get a hot candidate and you're eager to hire them. Word of warning. *Never, ever oversell the job.* It will only cause trouble. New employee arrives, doesn't get what was promised and quits. A waste of time and money AND it sends very bad signals to the outside world – where he is now talking about you.

Offer a future

However, do map out what they can expect and listen to what their hopes in their career are. Meet these as best you can, depending on their performance. Appraise them frequently and discuss how they are shaping up. Make them know how much you appreciate what they are doing. If you don't offer a vision of the future don't be surprised if they choose to make that future elsewhere.

Fight for their development

People need development. But they don't need it shoved at them. Too many companies push development at talent and wonder why they aren't grateful. Take time to agree a development program that can achieve what you both believe is best for them – then let them run it. Give them the budget. Make sure you make mid-course corrections and appraise how it is going. Try and use development ideas that will stretch their horizons and expand their experience.

Track talent that quits

Inevitably, you'll lose some people. Don't be surprised and don't be bitter. Often, people have reached the peak of their potential and, at the time, to make them stay would be to hold them back. Remember, if they leave you feeling good about what they have done, they'll be your best advertisement as a talent source. But, don't lose touch, there will be a day when you can use them again. And if you parted best of friends there is no reason, they won't come back if the challenge is right for them.

Steal from your colleagues

This one can make you unpopular, but what the heck! Often I see high potential talent being stifled by their direct report. If you see that think of ways to free them to come and work for you. Often it is a personality thing and the senior manager is relieved to have it solved in such an easy way. The stifled talent will be grateful and very motivated to show what they can do. Word of warning: don't do it too often, it gets you the wrong reputation.

Be flexible

This is the most important of all. Be flexible in your thinking, in your attitude, in who you hire and in how you let them work. Today, we cannot employ everyone under the same terms and conditions. If we want talent to work for us we must be open to new ways of working, new types of reward. Some talent will want to work part-time, others part-time from home. Others will want to trade bonus for vacation, have sabbaticals and so on. We as managers must be able to push for these things to happen, even if it means a war with a slow-to-adapt HR department; even if it means a dispute with your direct report. To be a place that is truly regarded as a talent magnet is tough. If we're not allowed to be flexible to achieve that, we're not going to get very far – are we?

"HE'S WORTH IT"

I have a friend who runs a small division of a large business. One of their employees – a very good worker – got into some serious financial problems, which resulted in a court order to sequester his paycheck at source. The manager asked the company to give him a loan to tide him over as he had both elder and child care to consider. The company refused. The manager went to the local store and bought him $200 of groceries and delivered them to the employee's front door. "It cost me yes, but he's worth it." The employee has since proved that over and over again.

Leadership traits in a talent magnet

I still have trouble with the word "leader" – and so do most employees. My cynical view is that the phrase "we want our managers to become leaders" is brought about on the basis that managers were told by their top managers what they had to do. They in turn told the rest of the employees what to do, and so life went on. Now in this complex world, top managers don't really know what to do, so they have hit on the brilliant idea of making managers leaders and telling them to go off and lead. Smart executives are not impressed.

However, there was a time when leadership was viewed as a less than discounted and devalued trait and I think it is useful to share this with any manager seeking to build a talent-driven department or business. In this there are six leadership categories and 35 leadership qualities. I think it is a useful addition to the talent magnet debate. I don't think it matters where you are in the organization, if you can do most of this stuff, you'll get recognized as a person who takes care of talent – that is the surest way of becoming a talent magnet yourself. People flock to work with good people.

The 35 Talent Leadership Qualities

Developing and communicating a strategic vision

- staying abreast of changing industry and market conditions;
- maintaining and understanding competitors' strengths and weaknesses, particularly in your own unit sector;
- understanding the critical leverage points of the business and how they affect your team;
- helping direct reports understand the company's business and objectives;
- developing goals and objectives that reflect the long-term needs of your group and the business as a whole;
- communicating an exciting vision of the future for your unit and the business as a whole.

Leading a long-term commitment to executional excellence

- establishing high performance goals and standards for direct reports;
- operating as a player/coach by demonstrating hands-on excellence;
- selecting and retaining the best people for your team and the business as a whole;
- working constructively with direct reports to improve their performance;
- relating rewards to results rather than seniority or personal relationships.

Demonstrating a responsive leadership style

- creating a sense of urgency in your leadership style ("let's do it!");
- deal effectively with multiple priorities and conflicting issues and help your reports do that;
- encouraging new ideas and alternative points of view;
- managing change in a thoughtful and well planned manner – rather than seat-of-the-pants, reactive;
- confronting conflict in an urgent, honest and direct manner;
- giving your reports a clear-cut decision or answer when they need it, not afterwards.

Creating a climate of individual responsibility

- giving direct reports the opportunity to provide input to the business;
- being clear and thorough in delegating responsibilities;
- expecting direct reports to find and correct their own errors rather than doing this for them (creating freedom for action);
- encourage innovation and calculate risk-taking;
- by taking the lead, encourage your team to stay close to the customer;
- reward people for trying new ideas, rather than punishing for mistakes.

Providing feedback and coaching for results

- being supportive and helpful in contact with direct reports;
- fighting for your people when you feel they are right;
- cheer on your people to greater levels of performance;
- provide ongoing feedback on career development;
- provide feedback that is even-handed, fair and "lifts" your people;

- regularly coach reports on how to succeed within the company as a whole.

Demonstrating high levels of integrity and honesty

- behaving in a way that demonstrates and communicates high integrity;
- being direct and candid in dealing with people at all levels;
- balance the achievement of short-term gains against the long-term business vision: shun quick wins;
- be seen to demonstrate a set of personal values based on honesty, consistency, feedback and trust;
- being willing to speak out or take on issues, even when your view isn't popular or welcome;
- demonstrating a balance between individual and team performance – being a good team player.

There's an awful lot of stuff on that list, not the sort of quick reference guide to keep in your pocket! So here's another angle: what do people expect from a leader of talent?

Leaders of talent

- listen carefully to what others have to say: taking the time to find out about expectations, needs and concerns;
- give or share credit with others, helping to build a confident trusting team;
- ask for, and positively encourage, input when working on projects;
- avoid becoming involved in "turf-wars" with other managers;
- understand and respect the personal agendas of other members of their team;
- solve conflict fairly and without emotion – they don't play favorites;

- keep people focussed on what the team is trying to accomplish;
- focus on issues and results not personalities;
- openly and quickly confront problems and different points of view;
- actively seek to find mutually acceptable solutions and never leave anyone feeling resentful;
- push constantly to make the team work effectively together;
- are willing to share resources under their control;
- are people who deliver what they promise above and below them;
- constantly seek win/win solutions;
- don't give up their position on an issue and fight for their people.

Begin to achieve and meet these types of expectations from those who work with you and report to you and you will be on your way to being a one-person talent magnet. This seems to work, even when the firm is having a poor time of it in getting the people thing right. How often have you seen a manager who seems to attract talented people, seems to get the best out of people and looks like they are enjoying it too? Those are people – although they may not put that label on themselves – who really are beacons for talent. They attract good people like moths to a flame.

Personal recipes

As part of our research into what being a talent magnet is all about, we asked our M-World respondents two questions:

- What is your personal recipe for making your firm or your own department a magnet for people?

And conversely …

- What is the thing that companies do wrong that really turns-off talent?

While many of these mirror our talent magnet criteria above, they are an interesting collection. Many were similar, here's a selection that might just give you more ideas of how you can become a successful magnet for talented people.

Remember, these are real people in real jobs right now, trying hard to track and trap talent. These are their "gut feel" reactions (you'll note the sense of some frustration in many!). Right or wrong, or no good for your firm, this is how real managers see it:

- provide a well-managed, friendly, learning environment for my employees;
- have fun, allow people to explore other areas of the company;
- smiles, helpfulness, eagerness, fostering independence – but help out as needed;
- increase pay, improve hours, make it fun and improve our reputation;
- implement new work initiatives, develop and empower employees, be flexible;
- dedication and responsiveness to others;
- honest treatment of people. Continuous effort of keeping them motivated;
- each employee being able to take responsibility;
- ask people what they want to do and let them do it;
- talk it up! Tell people it's great to work here and why;
- inclusion, challenge, welcome; flat organization that supports one another across department boundaries;
- creating innovative ideas and implementing them into successful solutions;
- to make my department a learning department;
- professionalism that is matched with equal levels of people and results orientation;

- value everyone's contribution. Recognize accomplishments often and publicly. Use the input that others bring to the table;
- build a team through training on the soft skills; developing and living the mission statement and vision;
- ask, listen: care about them and their families;
- balance the success of the company with the success of the individual.

Find a few things in there that mean something to you? Anything you can take away, or say "Hey, we should be doing that?"

Well, I am sure you'll find some of the things you shouldn't be doing in our M-World poll of what companies do wrong, that turns off talent. Strap on your seatbelt and read on:

- low pay and no opportunity for personal growth;
- put up barriers to learning and change and cease exploring possibilities;
- poor communication and feedback;
- stifle creativity and discourage personal choice;
- treat employees like objects;
- ignore employee suggestions for improvement without even considering them;
- no flexi-time, even when business can allow for it;
- keep employees waiting too long for decisions;
- too many rules and work/life out of balance;
- expect blind dedication without employer commitment to employees;
- assume that salary is all that is important;
- rewarding bad behavior and bad management;
- open conflict among members of management;

- treat people as a tool for achieving targets and nothing else;
- managers who micromanage and over-control;
- hire indiscriminately without in-depth interviews that will ensure a good fit;
- focus on entry-level jobs rather than career opportunities;
- non-performing firms that jump quickly into retrenchment and cost reduction rather than search for innovative ideas and solutions;
- use coercion as part of policy, while paying lip-service to empowerment;
- do not match positions with capable individuals and salaries;
- silo-style companies that restrict synergy and growth;
- expect people to be creative and work hard "just because we pay you";
- lack appropriate communication;
- a bad press.

DIGGING FOR GOLD

This story has been ascribed to a manager at Bechtel, the US civil engineering firm. Digging the new tunnel under Boston harbor the project hit some trouble. The manager recalled how he had heard of the same problems in New Zealand on a similar type of project. They located the – mainly Maori-workers, put some on a plane and put them together with the Boston workers over crates of beer. Talent helped talent. The manager didn't get cluttered up with the structure of problem solving, he created an instant social system where each side wanted to make it work and were motivated to do so.

Some questions for would-be talent magnets

Think you are ready to be a talent magnet? If you are, answer these questions and see how you would rank yourself. This is all about getting the confidence of people, getting their trust and making them better at doing their job. In fact, if you want your firm to be a talent magnet, why not get some of your fellow managers and team leaders to assess themselves too. There are no prizes for this except one: if you honestly feel you score high in doing these things then you are well on your way to being a magnet for talent.

How much time and effort do you spend helping your people make sense of their work and how it fits into the bigger picture? How do you do that? More importantly, how do you think they perceive you do that?

conversely …

- When was the last time you withheld knowledge from a co-worker to protect your status in the firm? What did that cost you? What did it cost the co-worker? What did it cost the firm?

- How approachable do you think you are? For example, when was the last time someone two levels below you asked you for advice either professional or personal?

- How much time and effort do you spend to get things done, to rally people around an unfamiliar or uncomfortable idea, issue or project? Do you shy away from these actions or not?

- When was the last time you publicly thanked and/or rewarded someone for their work?

- What do you really do to help teams, groups, departments and the firm as a whole to better integrate and operate? Are you active like this, or do you prefer to get on with your own job in your own unit?

- Finally, how long does it take your new employees to feel at home, to find out how things work, what is expected of them and where to get help and information? Do you help in that process or expect others to do it for them?

The talent magnet in trying times

Its relatively easy to be a talent magnet when business is running smoothly. Sales are up, profits are up and everyone's happy. Too many people want to join your firm, you have an oversupply of talent. But, that situation rarely lasts forever. These days a high-flying corporation can find itself in a crash-dive with all the engines on fire from one month's end to the next. That's when being a talent magnet comes under severe pressure.

I've discussed this aspect of trying to be – at the end of the day – a good manager when the going gets tough. Business down-cycles, mergers and acquisitions, a rough-and-tumble fight with a competitor all create concerns for employees at every level of the business.

While I was in the process of beginning to outline the idea of this book an interesting thing happened. All those telecommunications companies that had been the darling of the markets a few months earlier started to crash. Share prices slumped, redundancies were announced. There was fear and confusion all over the place.

I happened – by chance (as when corporations melt-down it is very difficult to get people's attention!) – to find myself in discussion with two senior managers from two telecommunications companies who were in trouble (one European, one American). Both of these were managers I respected, people who, I reckoned brought their fair share of talent to the firm's table and were able to keep it under most circumstances.

But this was different. Both were in lay-off mode. Both had – in the past month – said goodbye to close colleagues. They had – under instructions from on high – reversed the talent magnet's polarity. They wanted to fire, not hire. So, sounding a little foolish at asking them about talent magnets under these circumstances, I asked them "What do you do? Can you keep your reputation as a talent magnet (as an individual, or as a firm) if you have to go through this kind of unpleasant exercise?"

The encouraging fact was that they both said "yes." Well that was fine, but how?

This is my version of what they said:

- First thing. Stay positive and stay professional. Deal only in facts, don't add to the speculation of the rumour mill that will be working overtime;

- If you've got direct reports in far-flung places make a point of talking to all of them at least every 48 hours. You can reassure them, but don't make idle or empty promises;

- Make sure your direct reports do the same to their people on down the business;

- Deal with any rumors, concerns and other feedback quickly and without emotion. Above all, don't make promises and don't lie or "manage the truth";

- If the going gets tough, get tough too. Tell your managers that it is their responsibility to see this through for their people. Don't equivocate, be hard and very straightforward;

- Remember every day as you shave or put on your make-up that you can't be friends with anyone. Treat all the same, give them the same amount of time.

These two very professional managers say that if you are able to achieve that, you will do three things:

- not make enemies of people who leave (so they may come back one day);

- get the best out of those who are left behind, because they'll know you did the very best you could, but stayed totally professional;

- be seen as a manager who knows how to deal with good times and bad.

However, it can be tough, there's no getting away from that. One of these managers had to send out a collective e-mail to all his direct reports, reminding them in pretty hard-nosed language that they were managers and that they had to be seen to be looking after others, not concerned about climbing into the lifeboats first.

About mergers

Mergers, of course, screw up talent plans like crazy. People get reassigned, teams get broken up, some people quit, others get "managed out." Holding your team together in these circumstances can be very difficult indeed. Those that have been through it suggest a couple of points others may not have figured out.

- As in a downturn, keep your team as best informed as you can. Squash rumours fast.

- Get as much useful information as you can, but don't speculate. Reassure, but stay impersonal.

- The danger period is often when the first three months are over. Usually all the razzmatazz lasts about 100 days, the communications, the public relations, all that HQ-driven stuff. Then it goes quiet. That's the time you need to be able to hold your team together. So get ready for that.

And then of course the mavericks ...

More and more it would seem there is talent that needs its freedom to produce best possible performance. This is where our talent magnet manager needs to really understand what is meant by being flexible. In this, he or she is often faced with conflicting urges. Try and make them conform to some sort of corporate discipline and they will get frustrated and leave. Give them a totally free rein and others will leave instead. But we need these people. If our success as an organization is founded on ideas, then we need to embrace those that don't fit into the day-to-day mould of the executive. They need encouragement and enthusiasm for their ideas as much as the rest. They may be more difficult to understand, they may not make much sense at first hearing, but they should be listened to. Others in your group should know that these people are not "different", they are part of the team. Teams today thrive on diversity. It's managing that diversity that becomes the challenge.

Here are a few ideas given to me by managers that deal with maverick employees on a daily basis.

- Crazy as it may sound, make sure they know why they are coming to work each day. Do they have goals and challenges set for them? If not, do that. It focusses them on issues that they can deal with;

- make them a part of your group and let them feel "at home." Spend time with the others to make sure they understand that;

- make it clear to them that you welcome ideas – however bizarre, and you look forward to them;

- make time to follow up on a weekly basis on what they are doing;

- when they come to you, listen to the story, don't interrupt;

- encourage them. If the idea is not worth anything, try and get them to think about it in another way;

- don't cut them off or turn them down in public;

- don't say "I'll get back to you," and leave them hanging for a response. Say that you will consider it and talk to them in two days – and do it;

- never say "it's a great idea" when it's not, just to spare their feelings. By trying to build up their credibility you will lose your own;

- realize any odd-ball is just that until their idea works, then they are a genius. There was a nerd called Bill, he built a multi-billion-dollar company. I think it's called Microsoft.

DON'T PRINT THIS!

Occasionally, of course, even your best manager gets frustrated at the antics and errors of their staff. These are true performance appraisal comments collected over a long career.

- This employee should go far. The sooner he starts the better.
- His men would follow him anywhere, but only out of curiosity to see what happens next.
- When she opens her mouth, it is only to change feet.
- This employee has reached rock bottom and is starting to dig.
- I would not allow this employee to breed.
- He would be out of his depth in a puddle.
- This employee is depriving a village somewhere of an idiot.

Finally, think different

I'll bet that in your company, and certainly your division, the majority of people look the same. In fact they cluster together because they like it this way (more on that in Chapter 5). Is this a good idea? Is this the way to get a good spread of talent into your department or team?

Lately, as there has been increased pressure on the job market and the choice has been getting more and more limited, smart managers are realizing that they should start looking beyond the conventional for their talent. Being a talent magnet, a successful talent magnet, means being able to recruit, manage and retain a diverse group. If you can do that you will add to the richness of your team.

Just because the rest of your business recruits in the 30 to 40 year-old bracket, doesn't mean you have to do the same. There are a lot of very smart, very energetic 60 year-olds who know a lot, just itching for a chance to prove themselves one more time. Have a lot of males or females in your group? Why not diversify? As I have explained earlier, being flexible, and making the decision to do that can change how you look at the group you manage. Technology means that people can work on-the-road, from home, from customer's locations. Often this means that you can get someone who would never work for you five days a week (due perhaps to personal circumstance) who will do a great deal of good for your bottom-line by working from home for three days a week. Others want to job share, working mornings only, have the school vacations times off. We live in an increasingly unconventional business world. So, it seems sensible for us to embrace the idea in our employment offer, to be unconventional too.

Talent is everywhere, but it expects to be flexible and free. If we are to be successful magnets for that talent we need to help them achieve that.

5 Setting up the talent trap

The employer generally gets the employee he deserves.

SIR WALTER GILBEY

You can't hire part of a person. You get the sore back along with the skillful hands. You get the anxious heart along with the educated brain.

RANDALL TOBIAS

As we have already seen, organizing to be a talent trap isn't easy and it's not going to get any easier. We need the reputation and we need the people who are comfortable as acting magnets for others to join the business.

To illustrate that, here's an old story with a new twist.

If a boy meets a girl and he tells her how beautiful she is, how much he loves her and how he can't live without her – that's sales promotion.

If a boy meets a girl and immediately impresses upon her how wonderful he is – that's marketing.

But, if the girl seeks him out because she has heard from others what a fine chap he really is – that's reputation management.

What we need in our businesses today are people seeking us out, beating a path to our door, clogging our website with electronic résumés. And if we are not getting that, then we are definitely not a magnet for talent. But it isn't enough to attract warm bodies to your business. You've got to know which ones you want. Then you need to consider what will attract them to you. Finally, having decided all that, you can then begin to think about how to get them.

What we are going to do in this chapter is look at three things:

- What talent do you need?
- What does talent expect?
- How can you get better at attracting it to your door?

What talent do you need?

Ask most managers what talent they need and most will be able to tell you. Or, rather, they think they know. But, we have to be careful here. Times have changed and people have changed too. That word "choice" keeps cropping up all the time.

Remember our list in Chapter 1, the age groups? Well here it is again:

- Twinkies (still at college and under 20);
- Point 'n Clickers (20–25);
- Generation X (25–35);
- Middle-aged and Manic (35–45);
- Growing old Frantically (45–55);
- Grey Tops (55 and over).

… and it is here for a reason. Because we are going to have to think very carefully about our business and which of these groups we need to make our future plans become reality. Moreover, we are going to have to think long and hard about where we locate and how we plan our working days, if we are to get these groups to want to work with us. Perhaps we need a mix of all five employable groups, perhaps not. It is going to depend very much on our business and on different parts of the business with different needs from one another. Let's take a look at some examples of what I mean.

London's Soho, epicenter of the planet's new media scene. Talent galore squeezed into a few acres. If I am in that business, or in related fields like film, advertising and the cool-end of publishing I NEED to be here (at least with part of my operations). Why? Because this is where the best talent for this stuff hangs out. You'll also find it in Los Angeles, New York and Tokyo. But, and take this on board now, it is all in one area, in the city. And it isn't going to go anywhere else. Hot new media types do not go and take jobs in suburbs or greenfield sites close to airports. That is not what they were put on earth to do. Neither do they play by old-style employment rules. They come and go as they please, they party, they – heaven forbid – hang out with the competition. If you are in that business you need to know these things. You need to know it because the goals you set these people are going to be different from those you set your sales managers in an office park near Heathrow airport. These hot media types are going to quite possibly live within 100 yards of the workspace they occupy and they will eat, drink, have sex and smoke illegal substances in the same microcosmic little area.

It won't last forever. They are going to change. They probably don't know it yet but they are. Their values are going to change, their work patterns will change. If you want to employ them on a mid- to long-term basis you had better expect that and plan for it.

Why? Well they'll become other people. They form relationships, want to settle down, get a house in the suburbs or the country. What then? How do you deal with that, if your talent changes its needs and expectations?

The flip side of course, is that you might really want a bunch of nice, solid, professional engineers. You won't find them in the heart of Soho or Manhattan. No, you need to be located in a suburb where those over-spill areas sprout a thousand office blocks and glass-sided factories. You need to be where the talent can easily find you. And depending on your business and your future plans, your talent needs may either change or be a mix of talents. If you take that route you'll need a mix of places to play in. Because, mark my words, no 40-something engineer is going to schlep through the commuter crowds to Soho and no 22 year-old new media kid is going to feel that he has achieved his life's ambition in New Hampshire or old Hampshire, either.

Four views of talent management

All these cases actually happened. Only the names have been changed. They are included to illustrate the complexity of our business lives today and why we need new management skills to manage the talent we have.

Jim's story

A publishing company in the heart of London's Soho. There is a very, very, good acquisitions editor. He was single. He did live within walking distance of his open-plan workspace. He did meet his writers in a coffee bar across the street. He did hang out with the people he worked with (five of them even played in a jazz quintet together). Then something happened. He met a girl, he fell in love, they got married. She worked in publishing too, her name was Jane. They shared – uncomfortably – his one room, kitchen and bathroom. It had been fine when he was single and she spent weekends. Now it was full of her stuff too. It was cramped, it was stuffy, it was, what singles do.

They decided they had to move. Instead of hanging out in the bars, clubs and eateries, they wanted to have people over, have cosy meals together, have space. They started looking. They wanted to be able to keep the old habit of walking to work, or at least be close by public transport. They discovered, as many others do in New York, Los

Angeles, Tokyo, it was very, very expensive to get even a two bedroom apartment.

What did they do? They finally got a small house on the outskirts of town in a nondescript road, 10 stops on the underground. It may be home but it lacks the vibrancy, the excitement of their old one bedroom flat. So what's the plan? They are going to be on the move again. They don't think their joint income will allow them to buy in London for at least ten years (and there's a little bundle of fun on the way too!), so they are actively sourcing jobs outside the capital in places like Oxford, Cambridge and Winchester, where less cutting-edge publishing firms thrive and the housing is almost affordable.

But the lesson from this story is not that these people have been through a life change that has caused them to move. That's true. But what's important is that the hot-shot publisher in Soho doesn't know Jim is going to leave. Doesn't even suspect it. But Jim is a key man, a definite piece of talent he would fight to keep. But it is already too late. He hasn't seen the writing on the wall. Jim and Jane have entered a new phase of their lives. Jim's employer has missed that.

Lesson one: if you are to nurture talent know what it wants to do and where it is going. You can help people make the transition if you value their contribution.

Joe's story

Let's move on to New York. Joe is a vice-president for a large multinational. He has been all over the world. He is urbane, experienced, he looks like vice-presidents are supposed to look. Hell, his friends at the country club on Long Island say he looks like an actor playing the President of the United States. Joe's 50, his wife runs a local business near their home. He, of course, commutes daily to Manhattan.

In over 20 years with his firm, Joe has seen it all. He's 56, and has survived six major downsizings, two mergers and a heart bypass operation from which he has fully recovered. He and his wife have a condominium in Florida, where they intend to winter when they retire.

Lately the firm hasn't been doing too well. Hemmed in by aggressive competition and the subject of an anti-trust enquiry on a planned merger, the pressure is on. One weekend, Joe and his wife get talking. Their youngest child has just graduated and headed to a job in California. They own their sprawling house on Long Island and their home in Florida. Joe's wife Jill has had an offer for her business from a competitor in the next town. They come to a life-changing thought. Why wait to retire? We can do it now.

Joe goes to see his boss, who is taken aback by the news. Joe offers to stay on until things are clean and tidy and a new executive can take over. His boss, feeling aggrieved, says that's OK, and lets him go, quickly and without any fanfare. The boss thinks it is better that way.

Joe's, now ex, boss is a klutz. He has let a prime piece of talent walk off without as much as a thank-you (believe me it happens all the time). First off, if he had bothered to be closer to Joe he would have known that this could happen. Second if he had known and he had half an ounce of brain in his head, he would have not waited until ultimatum day. He would have made the first move.

Here is a fit, until now totally motivated, experienced employee, being let go when he could have been used in so many ways. And they should – if they understood managing talent – have been able to make him an offer. He could have easily:

- become an ambassador for the firm, woo new business, and hard-to-get customers;
- headed up a foreign subsidiary for two or three years and developed a successor;
- become a mentor to up-and-coming high potentials;
- worked part-time from home with e-mail and other technologies.

Lesson two: Today there are too few good people not to get to know what they expect out of life and then make them an offer that meets their needs and yours.

Jacques' story

Getting transferred from Paris to London at 36 was a great opportunity for Jacques. He is now heading up the marketing for northern Europe for his French firm, with an agreement that he can commute home every week, so that his two children don't have to change schools and his wife can keep her job as a pharmacist in a village outside the French capital where they have lived since they married ten years ago. He takes a small apartment in London, but he is rarely there: travel occupies three or four weekdays on average. Jacques and his wife have troubles. He is rarely home and finds when he is that they seem to be pursuing different life plans. He has been told that he has a great future with the firm. The next stop seems to be a major position at the Paris headquarters.

Lately, Jacques' absence from their home increases. Citing a lot of extra work, he often leaves on a Sunday afternoon and returns on Saturday, instead of Friday evening. There's a reason, and it's not all about work. Jacques has been spending time with his assistant, an attractive, intelligent, energetic woman of 27, who shares his enthusiasm for the job and his reawakened pleasures of city night life. Jacques decides that he will divorce his wife and live with his assistant in London.

With difficulty, Jacques explains a little of his situation to his boss. The boss is sympathetic to a degree, but demurs at getting involved in a personal matter. And things get worse. Jacques signs over the house to his wife. In turn he pays maintenance to her for the children. He finds he has little money left – certainly not enough for anything like the same sort of place he had in France in pricey southern England. Pressures mount, his work suffers and his new partner springs a shock, she has been headhunted to a job in Zurich and she's accepted it. A once high-flyer now spends his time lonely in a one-bedroom apartment in the center of London.

Again, a talented individual has been allowed to drift away, when it could have been different. The refusal of Jacques' boss to want to know personal details and get involved has created a crisis that didn't need to happen. In our business world today every piece of talent needs to be fought for. Jacques could have been counselled or at least given a lot more support from the firm. Right now, he is not only under-performing, but his only likely out is to switch companies, something he would probably readily do to build back his confidence and his badly bruised bank account.

Lesson three: Today, we all need to get involved and know what our top talent is going through. While we may find it difficult to pry into personal lives, getting to know more about those that report to you is imperative. We all lead complex lives so we do need to have some information of what people are likely to do, likely to want and likely to react to.

Janet's story

Janet is a 34 year-old single banker. She has built up a huge expertise through her willingness to travel, almost constantly. She has no apartment, no ties and is very good at her job. That job, for a New York bank, takes her for months at a time to former communist states, where she is part of teams advising on economic strategies to pro-free market governments. Her bosses love her. She works hard, never complains and delivers on time, on budget. They see her just two or three times a year, when she has lunch and a debrief at some wood-panelled club favored by the senior partners. She's even been known to puff the odd cigar! All they know about Janet is she is very good at her job, and her "home" is her parent's house in Boston, where she keeps the bits and pieces of her life.

What they don't know (because they either never chose to ask or didn't even consider it) is that Janet has a secret. Has had for some time. She has been very moved by some of the scenes she has witnessed in her peripatetic life. Poverty, people with unfulfilled hopes and ambitions, people trying to do better and being held back.

We need to know that we all have life changes and we all have them a lot more than we did. After eight years on the circuit and no expenses (apartments and living expenses are included) she has amassed a good size bank account, more than enough for a single girl to live on for quite a few years. She has always loved film, particularly documentaries.

Unbeknown to the bank, because they never showed any interest in anything but her work, she has taken every vacation for four years at a film school in London (it has been her only extravagance). Now she is a fully-fledged film director. Not only that, but through her contacts she has been offered a job with a documentary film unit: it pays peanuts, but she does-n't care.

Janet quits the bank to find if not fame and fortune at least extreme sat-isfaction and challenge. Her goal to begin to document former commu-nist countries' struggle to get their people to expand their horizons and better themselves.

Boy, was the bank surprised. Their, seemingly single-minded, single-purpose, workaholic, not ties-to-slow-her-down high-flyer was gone. Did they try and keep her? You bet they did. Did they offer her more money? You bet they did, and as many cigars as she could smoke. But it didn't work – never would.

Lesson four: If the bank had been smart it would probably never have come to this parting. If they hadn't been so self-centered and given her a vision of the future, or told her what it could be, she'd still be there. Never mind quitting for a low-paid job, they should have considered that she would get into a long rela-tionship at some time and then where would her choice be. Great talent doesn't have to be at the top, and they should have known that. Let's hope the share-holders don't find out how bad they are at talent management.

Ever more complex life-cycles

The reason for choosing those four cases was that I hope they illustrate that most of us in business today are trapped in much more complex life-styles than even a decade ago. Our expectations are higher, our needs are greater.

If we look back just a few decades what happened to the business executive? He or she (it was usually he) left college, got hired, got promoted, got married, had children and retired…. If the little men with their slide rules (remember actuaries?) got it right you died a few years later! What a simple, linear existence!

Today, things like that just don't happen. Yes, we have life stages, but they don't progress solemnly to a foregone conclusion. We have more freedom, more choice and we demand to be more flexible. So, what happens to our talent?

- 50 year-old executives divorce, remarry and have a second round of children. This changes their views on mobility for a start!

- other 45 and 50 year-olds decide to quit the rat race and start a whole new career;

- divorced women go back to work;

- 30 year-old women decide to stay single, work hard and play hard – that lifestyle demands a different view of work;

- long-term commuters rebel and demand to stay at home part of the week or they'll quit.

Talk about these trends to many executives and they'll shake their heads and think you have been having too many glasses of wine at lunchtime, or been smoking that wacky-baccy. But they are very real.

I am old enough to remember when the only 50 year-old fathers were ageing movie stars trying to keep the flame of their popularity alive through a late show of virility. Not now. I have to admit that I am a 50-plus father. And, since that event, I have been amazed at just how many others there are. My father-in-law is a 60-plus father, but he lives in California, so that's OK!

But it isn't funny or weird. It is a new way that we are living our lives – because we can. Because conditions allow us to. Because the social conventions of our parents' generation no longer apply. Why then has it taken so long for companies to realize this and get the simplest of ideas into their heads?

"Employees don't behave like they used to. They don't behave, period."

They are going to do this stuff anyway. If we want to be a magnet for talent to them, we had better have systems and policies and procedures that can embrace this change, that is now practically the social status quo.

What we have done is create bespoke, tailor-made lives for ourselves. Car manufacturers claim today that you can build your own unique model. By choosing what you want as options, colors and trim you can have the car that no-one else has. What they should add is that no-one has your life either.

HR departments need to know that. They need to realize that if you have 15,000 employees, none of them are the same. There are 15,000 unique individuals working for you. They know that. Do you?

There is no reason we can't meet the challenges that this implies. Technology makes it possible. Everyone can access technology one way or another, so creating individual development programs, benefit programs and the like isn't that difficult. Don't impose, listen to what those individuals expect. Everyone wants their own unique life. They do that by choosing the options, the color and the trim.

A look at life stages

Let's go back and look at those work/life stages again and see what they mean for us as we try and become talent magnets.

Twinkies (still at college and under 20)

Simply put, we need to get to these people now. There's no point in waiting until they graduate, we need to be talking to them and getting their interest while they are still open to career suggestions. To make that work, the first thing any firm that wants to snare Twinkie talent needs to do is understand what they might be looking for – and it won't be what excited their mothers and fathers. Oh no! We are going to have to come up with some pretty revolutionary ideas to get these guys and gals considering our business as a place to park for a few years.

One way to get their attention is to use recent recruits to your business, who just might speak something of the same language. If you can find two or three enthusiastic young employees who are really turned on by what you can offer them, you might gain some kudos. One of the problems with this group is that they have zero experience of business and don't particularly trust it. Also we have to remember that many of them – no matter how bright they are – don't read newspapers (and certainly don't read the business section), so they tend to get all their "news" from television and, more likely, radio. Radio's coverage of business is virtually non-existent. At best it will be a 20-second sound bite, usually as a consequence of some firm declaring 3,000 people jobless. This does not send the most positive message about working for private enterprise! However, that is often all they have to go on. Getting their attention is hard work, and getting their trust and possible commitment harder still.

The most successful methods seem to be allowing them to find out slowly. Let them visit and see what your business is like, enroll them on vacation-time jobs and work experience. Let them spend time with managers, shadowing them for a few days and finding out what they do. All this tends – for those who have tried it – to build interest.

What do they want out of the employment offer? Here's a few thoughts:

- honesty from you, no salesmanship, you can't "sell" the job;
- flexible work schedules and the ability to get time off;
- they will reject long-term promises, they want the deal now and they won't wait for it until "they prove themselves";

- a challenge that will keep them focussed, with frequent changes;
- as little supervision as possible.

Lord knows where we are going to get the next generation of managers from with expectations like these!

Point 'n Clickers (20–25)

Many of these are already in work, or just heading out of college and university. They have similar work expectations to those of the Twinkies. Only difference is they know more about what they want and how they think they can get it. Certainly there are still some who could be clones of their fathers and mothers, but that is a smallish group. Most of these people expect to have the money and the time off for three or more vacations each year, have access to a car and a good level of disposable income. While it is likely that they will eventually settle down, becoming more like the older generations they are replacing, talent magnet firms cannot afford to take the chance.

We will have to attract them by alternative methods of recruitment, and keep them by appealing to them and making work life fun and social. For many in this group, they will quickly discover that work life and the colleagues they meet will take over from the friends they made in school and further education. Most will build a large part of their waking life around the business, one way or another. Therefore, talent managers have to realize that they are in fact providing more than just a job. In many ways – more subtle than in the past perhaps – they identify with the firm and the job they do. So it is more important than ever to have the right reputation and maintain it.

One of the big dangers all firms will face will be the mobility factor. One of this group leaves and there is a good chance that others will follow him or her. So the game is going to be keeping groups and teams just as motivated as individuals. They might not think they act like that, but they do.

Generation X (25–35)

This was the generation that knew it all. This was the generation that everyone wrote about. Now it's getting old and things have changed. It has been through quite a lot these past five years. The really talented risk-takers have possibly been a part of a start-up or some new-economy operation. Even if they haven't, they have learned a lot about the realities of life. Of course, they have been lucky, because the economic conditions of the USA and Europe have meant that in their working lives they have always had a choice of employment.

Indeed, some of those early articles about Generation X, were – on reflection (and I was responsible for some of them) – pretty silly really. Suggestions that, "Generation X had no loyalty because they had seen what being loyal had done to their frequently downsized parents" were, frankly, rubbish. The reason they had no loyalty was they didn't need to. They could move around, learn a lot and not be tied to any employer. Something their parents would have done if they had had the same economic opportunity. One author wrote that Generation X was good with money, because they had to be, being left alone to get their own meals and groceries, while their parents worked late into the night. There is absolutely no evidence that they are any more wise about money than any other generation – but they do have the Pizza Express number tattooed on their forearm!

However, as I indicated above, the signs are that this group is slowing down the pace and beginning to put down roots. Hell, it's getting older like everyone else. Evidence from recruitment staff in Silicon Valley suggests that come 33 or so, even the most mobile in the workforce start to look around for a more permanent place to park their palm-top. A slow-down in the economy and a consequent reduction in mass hiring binges by many companies will help too. This means that we are going to find it easier to hold this group, en masse, than in the past. However, there are still major talent shortages out there, which aren't going to go away and we need to be mindful of that.

Middle-aged and Manic (35–45)

These are the people who are most worried about today and tomorrow. They have the most to lose, because they don't actually have that much. While the Growing Old Frantically Brigade and the Grey Tops have equity in stock and property, these men and women are still paying for all that, plus the specter of college education for their kids. At the other end Generation X is still finding out what all this responsibility is all about. Therefore, the way to turn-on MaMs to your firm is to give them what they need right now – as much security as they can get. And that is exactly what they are asking for.

Companies that are seeking specific talent, that has some track record, are willingly offering sign-on bonuses, and three-to-five year guaranteed employment. At the top end, employers keen to beat the rest are putting up golden parachute guarantees too. If you can make a convincing offer, that allows them to put aside their concerns and get to work, you'll have an eager member of your team sitting on the front step just rarin' to get to work.

Growing old Frantically (45–55)

This is the group, whose predecessors bore the brunt of the downsizing of the early '90s, and they know it, because they were around to see it. But they don't seem that concerned, except if a major recession comes along. As a lot of us know, we have rediscovered the concept that people who have been in business a fair time, just might know something and – almost more important – they might know some others who know a thing or two as well.

These GOFs are highly valuable, and the smarter ones know that. As a consequence they are beginning to flex their muscles a little and ask for the "little sweeteners" that improve the quality of life:

- extra vacations;
- part-time working;
- partial teleworking.

With the shortage of new talent becoming available, I think that companies who value the contribution of this group are going to have no choice but to give them what they want. Already companies are setting out to do just that in their advertisements and recruiters' sales pitches. So if we can't match them, we can't be a talent magnet. Equally, I don't think that we can afford to lose people who have the kind of experience that this group has. Experience that not only turns up on the bottom line, but can help others with less experience to achieve more. Right now, any company serious about talent should be having a senior management debate about the policies and procedures and the limits to flexibility to keep these people. Failure to act means that someone else will. They'll either get a better offer (yes, people steal 50 year-olds today!) or they'll go looking if they feel someone else will have more appreciation for their contribution.

Grey Tops (55 and over)

These people are practically fire-proof. They've survived clear-outs, mergers and the rest and they know their business inside out. If they didn't they wouldn't still be there (why has no-one worked that out?). They are savvy, plugged in and – if used correctly – a jewel in the crown of any firm. They can – if allowed – enhance the firm's reputation, boost recruitment and help retention strategies. Why? People usually believe them and look up to them. All this nonsense about "the young don't care about these old guys" is just that – nonsense. Any smart 30 year-old knows he can learn from an even smarter 55 year-old.

But again, they have the whip hand and they are beginning to exert it. Like the GOFs, they want to take it a little easier and they are demanding the same sort of attention. My advice – give it to them, but extract some promises too. Make them mentors, make them present at development and training sessions, make them go out on the road and help train your people and keep in touch with the customers of the same age group.

But, you need a plan

However, the only way to do all this is to create some sort of integrated plan so you can see just where your talent lies in the business. If you don't know whether you have too many or too few at the upper age bracket, how can you begin to work out what to do? If they want sabbaticals, can you afford to give them, will it disrupt the flow of work, will it upset others who don't get the option? Today's business world requires we manage for talent, to hire it and keep it. It also requires that we treat it fairly and openly. Without setting up systems that can track our talent and understand what it wants at different stages of its development and career curve, we are not going to get very far.

Being a talent magnet today means not being reactive to demands and sudden trends, but being proactive, to have answers and straightforward rules already in place that can meet those trends head on. As we are going to see next, demands and expectations are going to be ever more complex. Without rules we can't begin to be as flexible as we'd like to be. Rules mean that we can be flexible with everyone, but still be fair.

Welcome to the work/life balance debate

No-one knows what work/life balance really is. Everytime you ask, you get another answer to add to the collection. No-one, it seems, knows where it starts (or where it started for that matter) and what are its outer limits. What I am going to do in this section, is describe some of the ways firms are looking at what have come to be called work/life balance issues. Uppermost in my mind while doing this is to realize one thing: whatever you call these policies and procedures, they are not about being nice to employees. They are about extending the employer/employee contract to give staff things that make them better workers by relieving them of some of the stresses and strains of modern living. Let's keep that in mind as we go on.

To begin, so-called work/life balance doesn't always get off to a good start. Consider this view: a survey of 2,000 executives in the UK found that nearly two-thirds of women believe that "child-free staff are becoming resentful about family-friendly policies." Of the men polled, more than half agreed with that. The survey, by *Management Today* magazine pointed out that it is not only those with children who want a balance between a career and a home life.

In talking to a large number of managers, it is to keep the mothers happy that, so-called work/life balance initiatives usually start. In the race to hold onto talent and scarce resources, companies have been turning somersaults to make newly-minted mums feel that they can safely return to work. So it's, let's fund a crèche, or provide outsourced child care – that starts it all off. This can then quickly move to home-nannies for sick kids, allowing mothers to come to work or time-off at home with your laptop, without any penalties.

This culminated in possibly the most opulent corporate kindergarten in the world at the headquarters of Cisco Systems, who spent millions of dollars on a hi-tech hatchery, where cooing mums and dads could check on their little bundles of joy via webcams on their PCs.

With all this effort focussed on working mothers, you can see why there would be some deep-seated resentment building up in those that don't plan to have children. So, one of the first things to get right in any work/life balance initiative is just that – balance. Make sure all parties are treated with equal concern and all get something out of it, otherwise you are storing up problems for yourself.

Another issue, that needs tackling early on, is to make sure that individual managers don't start their own "unofficial" or *ad hoc* work/life balance (WLB) programs without anyone's knowledge. This can also cause friction between teams, task forces and departments. It's easy to fall into this trap. A high performer on your team is having personal problems. To take off some of the pressure, you allow them to work at home two or three days each week, saving the commute and allowing them to better structure their day. No matter how well they perform and meet their targets, it will cause comment.

Resentment can build quickly. "When he's not here, I have to answer his phone," is only the start. "I'm having to pay to commute to work, they're getting paid to stay at home," is another. If they are at home dealing with a sick child, it can get worse. "Why should I cover for them in the office, I don't get time off like that. It's her problem, she wants to be a mother, I don't."

Early on, when requests for crèches and other WLB items start to build up, it is important that the whole issue gets addressed by top management and that a set of basic guidelines are created so managers and supervisors know what they can and cannot offer.

For example, several companies I am very familiar with had requests for sabbaticals from employees. Sabbaticals are fine in some organizations where you can easily (or with limited disruption) take a person's work and give it to someone else or share it out. In a lot of organizations this isn't easy to do. Worse, you cannot give it to some, because their type of job allows for it, and not to others. Because of that, many firms have ruled out sabbaticals completely. Or, in other cases have said that, "yes," employees can have six months off, but they must go and do some work-related project, that the company can benefit from as well as the individual.

As you can see, clear, unequivocal, basic rules are the key to starting off on the right foot.

Having said that, while a firm may lay-down the rules of the WLB framework and set limits, e.g. no sabbaticals, there has to be an element of commonsense in all this. If you are an international business, with many offices, obviously what one location regards as important, would be looked on as anything but useful in another. For example, in Asia, most managers already have domestic care arrangements in place, either through maids or family, so offering a crèche is probably not seen as much of a WLB advantage, while it would be snapped up in the USA and much of Europe. Therefore you can set the big picture rules, but allow local managers to use their commonsense to deal with local WLB issues with a certain amount of discretion.

Here are some real-life examples, which show that WLB can be all things to all people, depending where you are, what you want and the local situation.

Car-park chaos

Most employees take a car park for granted. Not outside Brussels they don't. There, major multinationals including 3M, Toyota, ExxonMobil and IBM, are trying desperately to solve a major WLB problem that means, due to lack of local infrastructure, it can take up to two hours for employees to exit the car park at the end of the work day. For organizations who are definitely keen to be seen as magnets for talent it is an untenable situation. Indeed, they have been losing employees after just a few days because they can't get into, never mind get out of the car parks. Bizarre as the situation may be, having employees spend up to three hours a day sitting in their cars doesn't do much for an individuals WLB. They intend to solve it – soon.

It's about security, Senór

In Mexico, Sarah Lee Corporation found that the one thing locals wanted was better security, particularly a safe way to access money. In co-operation with a local bank they installed an automatic teller machine behind the company's security fence.

Train stop

More and more companies are taking intelligent routes to solving WLB issues. These include creating railway halts at the plant, allowing for easy commuting as well as shuttle-bus systems to local transport hubs.

Focus on foodies

Companies like Silicon Valley's Autodesk, have a large number of single employees who aren't into the idea of cooking when they get home. They installed a *cordon bleu* chef (headhunted from *Star Wars* creator George Lucas). The chef cooks take-home gourmet meals for the staff, and also bakes cookies and takes them around the offices in the afternoon.

"Do your shopping, sir?"

Also, increasing numbers of firms, eager to get the best day's work out of employees, are creating supermarket services, so that they can either leave a shopping list at reception and get it delivered or are allowed to shop online for groceries and other items.

"and what about your laundry, too?"

Companies, like mobile phone provider Orange, found that with a lot of single people, who were working very long and late hours that they were having a "hygiene crisis." Employees, especially male, were just not getting around to the laundry. So they set up a drop-it-off and pick-it-up service, that gets yet another worry off the employees mind.

... and the rest

Other services being lavished on pressed-for-time employees include, car servicing at work, dental and medical clinics, language laboratories, video and DVD rental, a book library, travel agent and general store.

Look for all these services to increase in the next few years as employers add more and more goodies in their bid to become and remain magnets for talent.

It all starts at the top

Of course, one thing to remember. Any WLB initiative should be not only sanctioned from the top management, but practised there too. If the CEO seems to be a part of it then it sends a strong signal down the ranks. While often due to sheer workload and a great deal of travel and meetings that just isn't possible day-after-day, anyone can make a start.

At one company I worked with, I had asked them, at the end of a presentation on talent issues and WLB, to consider the one thing they could do today that would improve the WLB equation for:

- themselves;
- their team;
- the firm as a whole.

We came up with some immediate thoughts, but the real pay-off was about a month later, when I saw the top management team again.

Firstly, albeit with some grumbling from the older executives, about "not needing to do things like this in the old days," they had taken a decision to embrace a whole range of WLB initiatives, "because we have to if we want to attract and retain people at all levels of the business." But that wasn't all.

Led by the chairman, they had thought – seriously – through my challenge about what they could do, as individuals, to quickly and easily improve WLB. The chairman had been goaded to consider his WLB by his wife, who, unknown to him, had kept a record of how many nights he had been at home over a one year period. The result was lamentable. He decided that he was setting himself a personal target of being at home – or on vacation – with his wife 150 nights a year. I have no idea how he is doing with his personal goal so far!

The head of marketing had also been thinking long and hard about this. As a senior manager with responsibilities in Europe, Asia and South America he was most often to be found at 35,000 feet on his way to or back from somewhere. He was aware that this put strain on his private life. What he decided to do was to make certain that when he was back at headquarters he would leave no later than five o'clock each day. And, despite a rather surprised look from his boss, he said he intended to stick with it.

They had all discussed what could they do, collectively, to improve WLB in the business? At the end of the day it was, really quite easy. The firm was known in the industry as one with a definite "long hours culture." They decided to do, at least a little bit, about that. They outlawed scheduling meetings after five in the afternoon.

I've no idea how they are getting on with that. As the chairman said at the time, "that doesn't mean there won't be any meetings going on after five, we can start one at four forty-five and it will go on well past five." Ah, but at least they are trying and they are sending out the right signals.

Four stages of WLB

What we can begin to realize is that WLB programs need to be given the go-ahead by top management and it helps if they begin to live at least part of them too. Additionally, establishing from the outset a clear link between WLB policies and core business objectives is not only useful but mandatory if it is going to work in the longer-term.

Most people who I have talked with on WLB issues reckon that there are really four distinct stages in developing these types of initiatives and programs in any organization.

Stage one

Child care, working-women's issues. As we have seen already, these tend to be the triggers that set off the need for WLB programs in the first place. It is at this stage that many companies stall, and get no further or fall into – dangerous – *ad hoc* unwritten agreements with employees.

Stage two

WLB as a part of recruiting and retaining staff. This is the point that most companies who are serious about WLB have reached. They have drawn up the policies, they have been blessed by top management and they are beginning – successfully – to see some return on the investment.

Stage three

Changing the firm's culture to totally embrace WLB concerns. This is where WLB champions and aficionados would have us all go. But this is a much more complex way of looking at WLB. It requires a lot of effort, organization and budget. Basically, what it is doing is saying that the needs of the employees are paramount and we will organize our company entirely to meet their needs through totally flexible and interchangeable working practices. This leads to …

Stage four

Where you totally redesign jobs and the workplace to meet employee needs and, hopefully, employer goals as well.

Few organizations seem to get past stage four, for all the right reasons, most of which are the sheer complexity of doing it and the concerns that your employees will turn into a group of "too free" agents. Where it has been a success is in start-ups and spin-offs, where there is basically just a blank sheet of paper. In that case you can design and deliver a completely new structure without upsetting and uprooting an existing culture.

Again, as I said at the beginning, WLB is all things to all people. It has become a bit of a mongrel word, a bit of a misnomer. To some it is a crèche, full stop. To others it is a whole new working-world culture. Both sides – and those in the middle – believe that whatever it is they are doing it will polish up their image and shape the perception of those they want to hire, as a talent magnet.

So how far have organizations got, and what do they see as useful WLB initiatives? The range is not only surprising but fascinating. Hopefully, these cases will give you some food for thought as you create or revise your own WLB programs.

The case for being Orange

We just talked about starting with a clean sheet of paper. Well that's what Orange, Belgium's third mobile phone provider did. The firm was created in 1998, and needed to hire people fast. They realized, in one of Europe's most conservative markets that they had to dare to be different. Their "sell", their employment proposition, was pitched entirely on the basis of WLB to attract the talent it needed.

Here's Orange's own explanation for what they planned.

The initial phase will open with full-page image advertisements in which human resources are presented as a "unique selling proposition" of the company. The intention is to give a feeling and an idea of what it means to have a job with Orange by means of the image campaign. "Imagine the job you always imagined", runs the opening advertisement, followed by a list of the job benefits that the company offers. These benefits are described in more detail in a subsequent series of advertisements. It is not only the approach which is original, but also the fact that these advertisements do not appear in the recruitment columns of the newspapers, but on other business pages.

It is only in the second phase, that advertisements will be placed in specific recruitment section with precise details of the required job profiles.

The underlying strategy of this campaign is to develop the credibility and attractiveness of the new company (corporate image) with regard to human resources before proceeding to the actual recruitment phase. The first stage will aim at another category of possible candidates, the so-called "finders", who are not looking for a new job, but who might have a latent interest. Hence the conscious decision to advertise in the ordinary pages of newspapers as the "finders" cannot be reached by traditional job advertisement channels. It is only in the second phase that advertisements will be placed in recruitment pages, where the readers fall into the category of "seekers".

The campaign has unexpected features in terms of both concept as well as style and creativity. Averse to techno-speak, this campaign seeks to address potential candidates in a straightforward and honest tone of voice and to take account of their expectations. What is also unique is the combining of staff recruitment with the development of the corporate image. The extensive co-operation between the marketing and HR departments and the hiring of an outside agency are testimony to this integrated approach.

And what did they offer?

Their advertising listed it: "Experience the job you really like"

- earn a good salary;
- celebrate New Year with an extra bonus;
- keep fit in our gym;
- let our masseur spoil you rotten;
- leave your laundry with us in the morning and pick it up in the evening;
- let us also deliver your shopping at work;
- don't worry if your child isn't feeling well, our babysitter will take care of him at your house.

… and, yes, it worked!

The case for cheesecake

Sara Lee Corporation is one of the world's most successful fast moving consumer goods companies. On every continent, kitchen cupboards and refrigerators are packed with their products. They are a great deal more than Sara Lee cheesecakes.

Their foray into WLB came as a result of research amongst their own employees and realizing that their long hours culture and deeply ingrained Midwestern work ethic (that worked equally well in Utrecht, the Netherlands HQ) were having an adverse effect on recruitment and retention. Their study of 100 Sara Lee top managers made them think too: "70 percent said that their work and personal life were not in balance."

What also got top management's attention was that WLB was identified as one of the top two issues in exit interviews of departing employees.

Without the luxury of a clean sheet of paper, the company decided it had to adopt some aspects of WLB anyway. It needed to be seen as a talent magnet and it needed to adjust its reputation in the marketplace.

According to Sara Lee there were four key drivers to adopting WLB policies all driven, ultimately, by the bottom-line: a tightening labor market; the increasing importance of human capital; changing lifestyles and attitudes and the need to manage diversity. They were adamant that this wasn't a nice thing to do, it wasn't paternalism, it was a hard-nosed, practical move to counter problems they were already experiencing. Accordingly, their policy summary on WLB reads like this:

"At Sara Lee we are committed to support our employees in achieving an appropriate balance between their professional and private lives. This balance is the responsibility of the individual, but requires flexibility of thought and action on the part of the organization. Our policies will focus on:

- Making work flexible (place and time);
- Offering support, referral and back-up services.

Sara Lee set themselves five critical success factors, without which they were convinced the program just would not work.

Clear goals and measures

Any business initiative needs objectives and measures of success, e.g.:

- reduced turnover;
- increased ease of recruitment;
- reduced sickness and absenteeism;
- enhanced company image.

Commitment

- if senior managers do not "walk-the-talk", line managers will never follow;
- policy must be owned by the board of management, not just HR;
- WLB issues must stay on the agenda;
- goals should be set, monitored and openly reported.

Cultural sensitivity

- principles can be established centrally, but execution must be local;
- culture impacts on many key areas: e.g. child care; support services (on-site facilities);
- local laws and tax implications must be considered.

Culture change

- don't expect results overnight;
- take every opportunity to put the topic on the agenda;
- use workshops to address real issues;
- encourage managers to "walk-the-talk";
- address non-compliance within business ethics program.

Integrate WLB into existing procedures:

- induction;
- performance appraisals;
- training programs;
- business reviews;
- performance awards;
- exit interviews.

Address the culture of long working hours:

Consistently excessive working hours = commitment and productivity

Or

Consistently excessive working hours = inefficiency, inability or under-staffing.

Highlight, evaluate and address.

Communication

- initiative needs to be "marketed" as a real business initiative;
- communication must be bottom-up as well as top-down;
- glossy brochures are not enough – open discussions are needed for awareness and understanding;
- the most persuasive tools are examples of success in your own company;
- case studies of benefits to individuals help understanding;
- WLB is very personal – it cannot, and should not, be dictated by the company. For some, balance is separation, for others, integration.

Sara Lee started by targeting "quick wins" – things they could do immediately to get the WLB initiative off to a flying start and garner employee attention. Here are some they identified:

- start pilot WLB programs in companies with critical issues to solve and openness to change;
- share successes;
- include existing relevant benefits in WLB policy documentation;
- flexible hours, based on a "trust" system;
- on-site facilities (e.g. bank, grocery deliveries);
- emergency leave days;
- provision for working from home.

As a legacy of the firm's long hours culture, they also had to deal with dissenters, who saw the introduction of WLB programs as the company "going soft." Here's how they tackled those issues:

Solutions to WLB not being seen as a "real" business issue

- build into business reporting schedules;
- ensure objectives are linked to financial benefits (e.g. training budgets, recruitment costs, cost of absenteeism);
- build simple, illustrative business cases.

Solutions to WLB seen as a cosmetic exercise

- create a demand for change in junior and middle management through open communication;
- integrate WLB into performance reviews;
- foster leadership from senior management.

Solutions to WLB being equated with working less hard

- address issue of "present-ism (I'm at work, therefore I am working, I'm not at work, therefore I am not working)";
- move towards rewards based on "output", not "input";
- pilot WLB initiatives and quantify productivity impact.

Sarah Lee says that their experience with introducing WLB programs into the organization are successful and appreciated. They say that they have six pieces of advice for anyone starting WLB projects:

- open discussion must be facilitated;
- everyone must be involved, not just HR;
- WLB projects need a central top management champion to ensure focus;
- start small and build on successes;
- quantifiable goals are essential;
- institutionalize by building into existing practices and procedures as far as possible.

Organizational overload

Building WLB into the existing organizational procedures is a very good idea. Several HR managers I spoke to say one of the worst things that can happen is to try and add what is seen by line managers as "another bloody thing we have to do from headquarters." Managers in the field are hard-pressed these days and the last thing they need is another initiative that takes away – to their mind – from getting on with the job. So, good advice is to try and use existing policies and procedures and add WLB to them.

Other examples of WLB in action

Eli Lilley has, what they term a "worklife" philosophy that is based around:

- no longer say "no";
- treat employees as individuals (one size does not fit all);
- cannot be a free-for-all, must be in line with business needs;
- determined by line management, employee and team;
- provide flexibility within the working life;
- on the spot judgement for flexibility must continue.

This translates into alternative working practices and breaks from work:

- part-time;
- reduced hours;
- job share;
- term-time working;
- phased return to work after maternity or serious illness;
- "V" time: voluntarily reduces;
- staggered hours;

- official home working;
- paternity leave;
- career breaks;
- sabbaticals.

Hewlett Packard has a full set of WLB policies that cover a broad range of flexible work options:

- compressed work week;
- flexi-time;
- telecommuting, including working from home;
- part time, including job share and job splitting.

They summarize their WLB working programs under:

- benefits;
- measurement;
- evaluation and conclusions.

Benefits

- employees have greater flexibility in managing their lives: including family and leisure, personal business, or just avoiding traffic jams
- HP gains by having employees who have their personal needs catered for and so are able to put all the required energy into doing their job

Measurement

On an individual and joint (employee/manager) basis, with a trial period and an agreement around the following questions:

- the effect on your team in meeting business objectives?
- additional equipment needed?

- "what criteria should be used to evaluate the success of your flexible work options (FWO)?"

Evaluation

- what are the anticipated benefits of your FWO?
- what is the plan for employee/manager meetings to evaluate how your FWO is going?
- a database is maintained with the information of all FWO being used, by type and area.

Conclusion

Flexible work options are widely used throughout HP in all functions to meet work/life needs. Each manager is responsible for supporting their employees in their requests, while at the same time ensuring that the business needs are met along with their own work/life needs.

At Ford Motor Co they have put in place a program that is not only WLB, but after work too. The firm and the United Auto Workers have agreed on an initiative that embraces child care, tutoring, recreation programs and clubs for retirees. In addition it will help with travel and vacation planning.

Under the plan, Ford will establish over 30 centers across the USA that will provide everything from emergency day-care for workers' children, preparation courses for college entrance exams, after-school programs for teenagers and day trips for retired Ford workers. It is estimated that these centers will reach a population of around 300,000 people.

CEO, Jacques Nasser has said that the centers are a great investment as they will help to keep people on the job, rather than rushing home to worry about their children. "It is an investment in the future of our people, it will help us attract a better workforce."

And at Deloitte Consulting and Union Pacific they have created a "nap-at-work policy" for employees. At Deloitte, you get a nap room, at Union Pacific, it appears you can just flop down anywhere and doze.

Here's the scary bit. Union Pacific allow their engineers and conductors to take sleep breaks of as long as 45 minutes, as long as the train is stopped and another crew member is awake!

Here are some more scary thoughts!

We started out this chapter with the intention of showing how companies are fighting the talent magnet battle, we're not finished yet. All the same, we do need a little light relief. So, let's turn to David Drugman of Bay Cities Research in Atlanta, who has some pretty good views about the philosophy of managers swept up into hiring-mode.

"Hiring managers", says David, "suffer from the belief that good managers will seek out your company and that all the best people naturally live within the hiring manager's zip [post] code. They also believe in the Easter Bunny, Santa Claus, Oz, the second coming of Elvis and the Tooth Fairy!"

Here's the lesson for you: the people doing the hiring needed to be well grounded in reality. The reality is that they are NOT in the driver's seat. Hot talent does NOT beat a path to their door. They will NOT snare it unless they work really hard at it (everyone has another – at least – possible offer elsewhere).

Setting the stage for hiring heaven

Another part of the talent magnet process is that if you want to hire well, you'd better have the managers who are going to do the hiring clued up about what you expect of them. Also you'd better make it easy for people to hire people, get rid of as much clutter, bureaucracy and time wasting as you can.

Here are some great ideas that you can consider.

Most companies continue to make it difficult for candidates to be hired (talk about shooting yourself in the foot!). You give them laborious and complex employment processes, bureaucratic administrative procedures, offer depressing communications and, just for good measure, some of you make them apply in several different locations for the same company! You seem conditioned to think that good people are persistent, don't have a life and will keep knocking on your door until you finally hire them. They won't.

Instead of laying back, taking the passive approach and waiting for top quality applicants to contact them, managers should be seeking potential new hires out themselves. Only by taking the aggressive and proactive approach will you attract the best and the brightest.

How can you do that?

Streamline your hiring processes and make it as easy as possible for new talent to find you in the first place and then to be brought on board. Audit your current hiring processes. Check for outdated forms. Do you really need all those signatures on the requisition… on the job offer authorizations? The task? Reduce your bureaucracy and speed up your processes.

Train your managers in interviewing, selection and decision making. Shorten the decision time to a minimum. Good candidates are too often lost when managers delay the hiring decision (or as we heard earlier demur from calling the candidate at all!). You should make offers to people who meet at least 70 or 80 percent of your requirements. If they have that, then they have the potential to learn the other 10 to 20 percent. If you don't make offers to these people, you can be sure that your competition will, because that's about the best you're going to get!

Managers themselves need to be trained and clued-up too. They may not necessarily be up-to-speed, in fact many of them rarely are. They need to understand alternative sourcing methodologies. Then you can approach the task of recruiting in a co-ordinated, cost-effective manner.

If you run them through a comprehensive training program and walk them through the hiring process (possibly by real-life example), managers will become a great asset and not a liability to the employment function.

Make sure that managers keep files on quality applicants, interviewed candidates and future leads. Be sure that they keep in touch with these people on a regular basis. When you need someone else, you already have a head start on the search and don't have to reinvent the wheel.

Don't forget to "close the sale." Too many employment and hiring managers make the offer and then wait, assuming that the candidate will accept. Be aggressive. Contact the candidate within 72 hours of your offer. Do they have further questions? Does their spouse or partner? Do they want more information on a particular area – the job itself or the organization as a whole? Make sure that the candidate and their family have all the information they need to make the right decision.

Remember, managers are paid to manage not recruit. They shouldn't care about how you find new candidates. Just as your company considers the manager and their expertise to design and build your products, you should be seen as the person with the employment expertise in finding and hiring quality people. If one of your managers thinks they can do the job better than you, let them try it!

However, a well trained line manager can be a strong ally.

Make sure that your top team is committed too. Do they really have the work for the people you are going to recruit? Do they have the facilities (desk space, parking etc.)? Do they have the resources (money, computers, software etc)? Have they communicated all the way down to the first line supervisor (i.e. the manager)? There is nothing worse than a top executive hot to hire and the supervisor saying "How? I can't cover the people I've got now!"

The most effective way to hire a candidate is to get two people talking – the manager and the interested applicant. Interviews make offers happen, résumés don't – so make interviews happen!

It is easier to hire someone who already has a history with your company (e.g. former employee, one-time interviewee, someone who declined an offer etc.) than to try to sell to someone who has no idea who you are or what you do. Those who have a history with the company don't need to be sold, so they are more likely to accept or reject your offer sooner. This is known as "relationship" recruiting: it means staying in regular contact with targeted, qualified candidates. These are sources that only someone inside the company can take advantage of. Head-hunters and employment agencies don't have access to these sources unless you give them to them, and you shouldn't. This front-end work and data gathering also generate the highest quality candidates – those with a track record who have worked with you before and know your company well – in the shortest possible time.

You should introduce a formal process to review any or all employees who have been caught up in a company lay-off activity, downsizing or re-engineering process over the last 12 months. You might also want to look at lay-offs by department that occurred during the last three years or so to increase the draw from this source.

Make sure managers review this list before you contact people, to be certain they are all employees that they would like to have back. This should be done without any attempt at determining whether the former employee is currently employed or wants to come back. Stay focussed on the question, "would my department want him back?" The objective is to identify at least 5 percent of the list as being potentials for re-hire.

If you ran an outplacement initiative, or had one run for you, you should be able to get copies of your employees résumés that were created during this process. You can match the "wish-list" of potential re-hires against this. And get the good matches back to the hiring manager for review. If everything is still favorable, contact the ex-employee and let them know of the employment opportunity. If they are interested in the opportunities, it should be plain sailing from there on. Indeed, this should be carried out before any external hiring initiatives are begun. When the manager arrives in your office with an open requisition demanding action, hand him their historical lay-off list as a starting point.

Retirees

Run a list of recently retired employees by department, in particular highlighting those who took early retirement to give to your managers. Again, ensure that those on the list are employees that the manager would wish to have back. As above, the goal is to have at least 5 percent of the list as people your company would like to re-hire.

Job posting

Job posting is usually responsible for 5 to 10 percent of all positions filled within a company. These are current employees (perhaps at a different location) who are looking for new challenges or promotion. They would be internal transfers.

Companies use different methods of job posting. Some simply photocopy their open requisitions and put in various places around the office or site. Others include them in their intranet, internal newsletter or information brief. This is also the starting point for an employee referral program.

You should ensure that all openings are open to all employees all the time – and that they can be accessed as easily and rapidly as possible. Employees can also use these documents in their employee referral efforts to attract new hires from the outside. Often, they can find themselves in the hands of the competition, posted on their bulletin boards and passed around their offices. All the better. Ensure that appropriate opportunities (and that may be all of them) are available via your website on the internet.

Do this sort of exercise diligently and rigorously and you'll be surprised just how many people you can recruit without the costly intervention of external recruiters and search firms.

Some final thoughts on being ready to recruit

There's one thing disturbs me in a lot of this, being ready to recruit and work/life balance stuff – don't think we want to be too eager. I feel it is very necessary that every organization – no matter how much it wants to become a talent magnet – makes it clear from the outset that they are not some charitable institution. Often I hear stories, that in the race to recruit, hot candidates get made all kind of offers and promises that the business can never hope to meet or live up to.

Let us remember that employees must also be expected to live up to their side of the bargain, to be responsible. I feel that today, there is a group of employees who don't seem able to come to terms with that. Certainly we are in a fight for talent. Certainly that fight, that battle will get harder. But we want the people we employ on our side helping us to fight. Not sitting thinking what they can get out of us next.

Let us also remember that what one of us views as good practice, is possibly the opposite in another's view. I was at a conference, listening to a senior manager from amjaor corporation give a presentation on work/life blance. It was a good presentation, full of rich, how-we-did-it content. The audience looked happy, busily taking notes. At the back a man stood up and shouted a question at the presenter:

"Do you give them mobile phones?" "Yes", said the presenter. "And do you give them laptops too?" said the questioner, who was by the time becoming quite agitated. "Yes, yes, we do," said the presenter. "Slaves, slaves... you're turning them into slaves!!!!" screamed the man at the back, as he was quickly removed from the room.

An extreme view perhaps, but let's look out for more extreme views in the months and years to come. As the talent squeeze bites, so will the people be squeezed.

6 Other aspects of talent magnetism

There are all kinds of employers wanting all sorts of servants, and all sorts of servants wanting all kinds of employers, and they never seem to come together.

CHARLES DICKENS

Treat people as if they were what they ought to be and you help them become what they are capable of being.

GOETHE

Being a beacon for talent, I have already pointed out, isn't easy. Neither will your beacon stay the same for long. Both external and internal forces can quickly change the way your organization is viewed. Employees have little real trust left and will leave when they want, not when you decide. Externally, your reputation can change at the drop of a newspaper headline that indicates all is not well.

And, let's face it, other issues can impact and quickly change all the hard work the business has done to become a talent magnet.

Recently, I witnessed two organizations destroy their image in a matter of months, both through disastrous appointments of new CEOs: one who seemed not to understand the business and the other who was hell-bent on widespread change and never mind the consequences.

You know it is getting bad, when people with ten and more years tenure voluntarily quit, and that is what these two CEOs managed to achieve – organizational meltdown from the inside out. Sometimes it seems you should have a licence to practice before you become a CEO.

Equally, you know it is already bad when the organization fails the car-park test. This is an easy litmus test on the real health of any business. All you have to do is look out the window and see how many cars are still in the parking lot at five in the evening. If yours and the CEO's are the only ones there, then it's time to drive out the gates and not come back. I have seen this time and again. Today's employees don't walk out, they drive out with their foot firmly on the gas pedal. In Frankfurt, a car park empty at eight-thirty in the morning and filling up by five after nine: that's a sign employees don't care. In Amsterdam at three o'clock on a Friday after-noon they are pouring out the exits AND the entrances in their eagerness to get out of there. You don't need consultants to tell you that you have troubles, just use your eyes to see and your nose to smell the tyre smoke!

Is that a little excessive? I don't think so. No-one's going to be fooled these days. Everyone either knows the share price or has access to it. Everyone can access the internet and find out what the analysts and others think of the company you are employed by. And everyone can spend coffee breaks and lunch times eating a sandwich and getting a new job using your PC: and they do!

Can we do anything about that? Not when the rot has already started, no. The atmosphere is already created, there has been a culture change. Everyone is in "me, me, me" mode.

The Nokia Way

The plain fact is that we need to invest in the good times for when the bad times come along – because, no matter what we do, they most surely will. How bad they are, is based on how much time and effort you put into building a loyal and happy following. And that means that you need to face the reality that sometimes – for all sorts of reasons – you will have to let employees go. How you do that though, reflects on what others think of you and your ability to maintain that image as a talent magnet.

Consider this: when the telecommunications and mobile phone industries were busily shaking themselves to pieces in early 2001, they all got a pretty bad press – except one. Nokia.

Okay, they did seem to weather the crash better than others from a numbers point of view. But why was that? Wasn't it, deep down, because they just managed their talent better and were able to organize to meet the threats and challenges they faced? Weren't they able to get a faster, more intelligent, more productive response to the crisis from their employees, than Ericsson, Motorola and Siemens? Personally, I think it was, and I think that every manager in every industry can learn a lot from that.

What's interesting is that their CEO (I've already referred to this earlier in the book) spends a lot of his time explaining what they now call "the Nokia Way" to others. He sees this as part of his job. Fact is that Nokia has been phenomenally successful in bringing together people from diverse cultures, backgrounds and geographies and uniting them into one cause, the Nokia Way. I know others do it too, but, possibly not quite as well.

Nokia's CEO Jorma Ollila, sees this Nokia Way as being all about the ability of the firm to get this diverse mix of people to sign-up for the same set of values. Not only that, Nokia has tapped into the fact that, as Ollila says, "values are extremely important to the youngsters of our era." He adds, "the winning companies of the future will be those who can attract the best people, and to do that a strong value base is essential."

Nokia's belief is that you can have a family-based culture that is built around values, attitudes and management behavior. But part of that has been a decision – followed by an active program – not to get any larger in terms of people. "If you look at companies of 100,000 people and those of 50,000 people, you'll find that they are very different," Ollila has explained.

Nokia, has a lot of young people. Twenty thousand of them are in research and development and all have their own ideas and expectations. That's why the firm felt that establishing values that this dynamic group could subscribe to was going to be vital.

Their values are based on the following:

- speed and timing;
- openness;
- integrity;
- teamwork;
- humbleness;
- accountability and responsibility;
- empowerment;
- tolerating ambiguity.

A lot of commentators have said that Nokia's success happened because it was a Finnish company that set out to replicate its values wherever it worked: that it wouldn't have worked for others. I'm not a subscriber to that view. I think any organization, anywhere could do the same thing if they wanted to, it just happens they don't.

Much of what Nokia did is already in the early chapters of this book:

- senior management worked out who they wanted to hire;
- they created a set of values that their target group can fully buy into;
- they unswervingly lived those values and "walked-the-talk";
- they constantly tinker around with the model to make sure that it doesn't get sterile but stays dynamic and meets the changing needs of the business and the people in it;
- they promote the model – and the results it brings – as their talent magnet.

The only reason that other businesses don't do that is because:

- senior management don't "get it." They are not aware of what the generations want and still manage everyone practically the same way;

- they have a set of values (they think), locked in a planning manual somewhere, but they don't walk-the-talk much – more like hop around on one foot occasionally;

- they can't tinker around with the model of their values, because they've forgotten where they put it. Consequently, they have different values for different groups and differing businesses;

- they send out a series of confused, muffled messages about who they are and what they expect from employees;

- they don't promote a model, instead they spend millions on global image advertising, that only confuses current and prospective employees further, but the chairman and the CEO love it!

Cynical? Yes. Can't be like that can it? Oh, grow up! For a huge percentage of businesses, I've just described reality. The trouble with reality is, it bites you – HARD!

Goodbye, goodbye, we're leaving you goodbye!

Reality bites really hard when good people – as well as those you have hoped and prayed would one day seek other work – decide to quit. Just like the photocopier that runs out of paper, or the stapler that runs out of staples, they always do it at the most inconvenient time. But unless we decide that we are truly going to be a talent magnet like Nokia, we are never, ever going to get control of this precious commodity known as people.

So, it isn't enough for the chairman to have a sudden vision in the executive washroom that all is going to change and you are going to be born-again employers that truly set out to meet real needs and expectations. Your offer, your day-to-day values are going to have to be exceptional, if people are going to stay for any length of time. Think all those people are so happy at Nokia, that no-one leaves? Forget it, of course they do.

Throughout this book, I've been talking about people being attracted to your business, but it might just be useful to spend a few pages considering the opposite. Why do those people that once were happy to join you want to quit. As with everything else today in this complex business world, there's more than one reason.

There are really two types of reason why people decide to leave: professional issues and personal issues. As I said earlier in Chapter 5, there's no point in concentrating on being a great employer if you haven't a clue what a key manager's personal life is all about. You are only responding to half of his or her needs and wants.

Career issues

Let's start by looking at career issues that prompt the one-way drive out of the parking lot.

The new boss

As I have just described, this can trigger a quick exit for people who think they were passed over for promotion and there's no future, a major personality clash, or simply different ways of doing things. The other side to this of course, is that the new boss may want to remove some of the people before they can cause him or her any trouble. I know a manager – usually sent into problem situations – who has a policy of always firing at least two people in the department or division he inherits, "just to send a message to the rest that we are going to do things differently around here." While not, perhaps, the friendliest way to start off, it often works – short term. After that sort of beginning you are more likely to be watched with concern for what you might do next than loving affection.

Endings

The end of a project, task force or team can also provoke defections. If you haven't made it clear what people get to do next, they'll go looking on the outside. Equally, if they have had a fascinating challenge and the next assignment is nothing like that at all, it means that you are playing poker dice, and running out of options. Add to that, the other great quitting category, which is returning expatriates. A staggering 60 percent leave within two years of coming back to headquarters, mainly because they don't get the kind of work that meets their new-found experiences.

Three year itch

People who job-hopped used to be regarded as unreliable, but that is just not true anymore. Firms want people with a lot of different experiences and the way to get that is to move around. The weird thing in all this is that while we are spending anxious hours trying to hold onto talent, we are also trying to poach talent from others that hasn't been left hanging for too long. But again, it shows that we are very much in a different world, where we need to keep a close eye on our people – especially those that absolutely MUST stay. Managers and HR should have systems that begin to warn of impending doom after 24 months goes past.

Not getting the assignments they want and perceiving themselves as being held back will also engage the trip wire. My view is that we must move people up – or challenge fully them – as quickly as possible. If we don't, we will lose them. Additionally, not getting a raise, getting a meager bonus can both be time-to-go triggers. In these times of shortage, you can almost guarantee you can get more money elsewhere, if that is all you want. That is also, conversely, another reason people quit: new fires being brought into the company at much higher levels of compensation (we'll get to pay later). This, sadly is almost inevitable as the market for scarce talent moves upwards.

Personal issues

These days, there are a lot of different reasons why employees, often, on the surface, completely happy, motivated employees, suddenly surprise you and quit. While you can't predict them all (today's life stages being so mixed and often messy too), getting to know the employee better certainly helps.

Family bereavement

This can bring about all sorts of reasons for the employee needing to seek a change. Possibly all that anyone can do is be as sympathetic and helpful as possible, perhaps offering to hold open the job, or work-out some part-time or out-of-office working solution. Of course, in some situations this also results in an employees inheriting an estate, which can bring about (more and more these days) major change in their lives as they may well find themselves independently wealthy. I have recently seen this at first hand (not me personally, so no letters please!), where an intelligent boss, was able to get a very valuable employee (who had just inherited two million dollars) to continue to represent the company to give him, as he put it, "an interest." While this won't work for many, it just might work for you and is worth considering. In reality, it is no different from getting an ex-vice-president to do the odd bit of work after they have retired.

Inheritance aside, we are now in a world where most employees play the market and some get very lucky! Again, think about whether offering an employee, who appears to be set up for life, some part-time work may be a good idea.

Illness

Illness, particularly serious illness is the other issue that cannot be predicted. This can be especially hard if it is an close family member to the employee, where they do need to take time off to be with them. Again, it depends on circumstances, but most companies today will think long and hard before they just let someone go on these grounds.

Marriage/divorce/children

Many more people have second, third and even fourth marriages these days. Each one of them triggers a new cycle, and means that your employee can quickly change their entire view on life – and work too. Divorce creates another cycle as does the arrival of children. All these life events mean that priorities change and they affect the job that the person is doing. Equally in these days, you can find that the act of children leaving home can create new freedoms or wants that have been buried in your employees for a long time. Whether you can suggest they do their job from Florida or Southern Spain remains a choice for you to make!

More about pay and reward

While we can't get into the technicalities of pay here and certainly can't look at pay scales, it is important for managers to understand some of the major trends that are taking place. Without this, you will be unable to make the right kind of offer, or take the fight to your HR department who are muttering darkly about "exceeding budget" and "creating precedents" with the package you are about to offer some hot-shot prospect.

To begin, let's consider – for the purposes of explanation – that there are three pay categories we need to concern ourselves with:

- the exceptional: wow-factor one!
- the, ooh, yes please!
- the mediocre.

The mediocre

This is 80 to 85 percent of your workforce. They are unexceptional. Loyal, yes. Happy, yes. Exceptional, no. You can hire lots of them. In fact you could go to most of your competitors and swap over 80 percent of your people with their people and it wouldn't make any difference to your business. Not one iota. While many might take exception to that, think about it. It's true. But we need the mediocre. These are the horses of the business. They are strong, but are not going to set the world on fire – ever. They will pull and pull the business along. However, you have to keep turning them and pointing them in the right direction. When it comes to pay, you give them the going rate. If they don't like that they may get more somewhere else, but it won't be much more and they are with you for more than money. With this group, the social factor counts high and they are often – too often – reluctant to move on.

The, ooh, yes please!

This is the 14 percent who make your business what it is, and by judicious acquisition, will make it better still. These are the people you must never, ever let out of your sight. Only the rule of law stops you from chaining them to their desks at night. What you are going to do with this group when it comes to rewards is pay what it takes, because, they'll do the job you want and more! This is the group that gives the HR department conniptions. Because, if you want them, they are not only going to cost you ('cos they know what they are worth), they are going to screw up HR's neat little salary ranges and progression curves. But if you don't hire them, your competitor will, and then where will you be? Additionally, news will leak that you have hired this person at 20, 30, 40 or 50 percent more than anyone else at that level. The entire department goes home sulking and dusts off their résumés. If you did that, you got it wrong. If HR or the CEO let you do that, they got it wrong too. What you do is, think out of the silly little box with the job tag in it and the accompanying salary range. The rule is, "hire the person, don't fill the job."

This IS important. If you try and fill the job you are attempting to find a person just like the one who just quit. That's impossible. In today's world, where everyone wants to be – and intends to be – different at work as everywhere else, you cannot hope that any attempt at corporate cloning will work. What you do, is get the very best person you can and expect them to do more than the person who left. Then, don't stick them in that salary bracket, tell HR to find another one!

We must not get bogged down in trivia if we want to attract and hire talent. Dickering around trying to get permission to go over the salary guidelines does one thing. It sends the wrong message to the candidate and if he really is in the "ooh, yes please!" category someone else has already said that to him.

Pay the person, not the job. It needs to be your mantra, otherwise you'll never get anyone good and you certainly won't keep them.

The exceptional: wow-factor one!

These are rare birds indeed. They don't come onto the market often and when they do there is usually a punch-up about who gets them. But, if you've got two or three around they are going to make your business hum like never before. We are not talking necessarily top management here, we are talking of people who are very good at something, are leading-edge, are practically the best there is. They are the best logistics guy in your business, the best government negotiator in the global Telecomms market, the best seismologist in the oil and gas industry, the best e-business expert in banking and finance. They are not that visible outside of their industry and specialization, they never get onto business magazine covers, they are just exceptionally good. You want them, they make you money and they save you money too. You don't say, "here's the salary" you give them a bonus based on what they do. Which brings us to the next part…

The global pay-packet

At the "wow-factor one!" level you pay whatever is needed to get the person on your side. Because if they are not on your side then they are the enemy, because they are going to be working against you. This is the level of person where, if your bunch can't get them, the "A" word, as in "assassination", crosses the CEO's mind, in the bleak wee hours of the morning when he can't sleep. And wherever they work, they get what they want.

Down at the "ooh, yes please!" category, we are seeing the rise of the global pay-package. Whether you are in New York, London, Zurich, Hong Kong or Moscow, you are (with the exception of local requirements) going to see roughly the same amount of loot for the work you put in. At the same time we are also seeing a great increase in all sorts of split payments, as the lawyers try and work out how, legally, you can pay people large amounts of money without incurring huge tax penalties and massive social security contributions.

The smart job-seekers today, are basically saying, "look, this is what I want in my pocket. How you work that out doesn't concern me. If you want me to join you this is what it will take." Again if we can't make that happen, we are going to be batting in the minor leagues.

How much can head-hunters help?

In our bid to be a magnet for talent, can the head-hunters add anything to the party. My view is, yes and no.

- Yes, because when you find a good one they are very good indeed;

- No, because unless you can tie them down tight, they'll get busy and some second-rate operator will be doing your searches;

- Yes, because if you build the right relationship and make them really understand your business, they will be a great ally and will find people you never could;

- No, because most of them can't do that because they don't have the hands-on industry experience to really make a difference.

Anyone who expects head-hunters to be a one-stop solution to securing talent is going to be disappointed. In today's world they are under more pressure than ever to deliver, quickly and without too much fuss. In defense of the head-hunter they are often ill-briefed and frustrated by too little access to senior management.

Having said that, there are cases where senior search professionals – often with a good grounding in big-business life – develop long-lasting relationships with CEOs. At that level, they can make a difference. They are objective, they can say things members of staff can't say and they can look under a lot of rocks the business can't. They can also approach a lot of people the business can't.

I've had a lot of associations with search firms over many years, and my advice to any manager is, assess the firm on the basis of what you want them to do for you. If you have a lot of work at mid-level, get someone who can do that and has the people to do it. Draw up guidelines and rules and stick to them. If you want special people at the top of the business, if you require to seek out the very best, then get the very best search people to help you. But don't settle, ever, for second best. If the guy at the top can't do it, try somewhere else. The biggest complaint I heard in 1999, 2000 and 2001, during the boom of talent chasing, was that the search firm had assigned a second or third class person to them as the principals were all too busy. Don't let that happen.

The other advice is, don't sign exclusive agreements with large firms who claim global coverage. Even if they do (and that is, at best, doubtful, they may have "correspondent" offices) experience will be patchy. No firm, anywhere, has on-the-ground expertise in every country and region that covers every industry. Beware, beware, beware.

Instead, if you are serious about hiring great talent, build up your own black book of really good local firms, or even individuals, who know your business and the players in it. Don't rely on directories, they are notoriously inaccurate in my experience. Use your head and your phone. Call a few colleagues in other companies and find out who they recommend. That way you can use the best people in any given situation.

Like everything else, it all comes down to "you get out of it what you put in." Too often I hear managers saying how disappointed they are when all they did was pick up the phone, have a 15 minute meeting and then, ludicrously, expect the greatest candidate of all time to walk in the door three weeks later.

Finally, one last point in dealing with head-hunters. As I hope I have shown, there are new needs and expectations on the part of the hunted these days. If you are going to use a head-hunter or a recruiter for those low to medium level hirings, take the time to check out that they know what you are looking for and that they understand the real expectations of today's employee.

Don't forget your own people

I've touched on this a few times already, but it seems a good idea to repeat it here again. The best advertisement you have – assuming they are not in open revolt – is your employees. Therefore, use them to snare candidates, and reward them well for it. This is an easy way to get people who will usually fit in with few difficulties because they will, most at least, be like minded individuals. It is also a very cost-effective way to hire-in, even if you give employees $3,000 every time (make sure they last at least six months, before you pay the bonus!).

I consider that in every switched on business, every employee is responsible for attracting and retaining talent.

Getting talent onto boards

When people talk of being a talent magnet, we tend to think of hiring and holding onto valuable employees. But increasingly, in an ever more complex business world, smart corporations are investing in external help from senior managers in other organizations. As companies seek a competitive edge, carefully selected non-executive directors are becoming valuable intellectual currency that few globally operating organizations can do without. They also send a message to the marketplace. "If you can get these people to join you, you must be a good organization, worth at least a second look."

There was a time when most non-executive board members were composed of the chief executive's golfing buddies or tennis partners – possibly leavened with a business school professor, a member of a minority group and, more recently, a woman. Photos in annual reports tend to be the same the world over, sober-suited, white-shirted, carefully chosen tie. At least in the USA there was a photo, in most European and Asian annual reports, there was a simple list of the directors in anonymous – equally sober – black type.

But as globalization speeds up and more and more companies seek to trade in every corner of the world, the CEO's friends are more of a liability than anything else. What is needed (particularly to build the perception of being a talent magnet) is bright, experienced business people that understand the global economic arena and the best ways to capitalize on it.

If you are going to do business in Asia, might it not be useful to have an up-to-date Asian expert from a leading corporation as a non-executive director? If your plans call for cross-border acquisitions or mergers, isn't it important to be able to get sound counsel from someone who has been there and done that?

Mergers like those of Upjohn/Pharmacia, Daimler Benz/Chrysler and BP/Amoco, Deutsche Telekopm/One2One; Air Liquide/BOC, all require an encyclopedic understanding of how boards in one country and culture differ from another (e.g. in the USA and Britain, directors are responsible first and foremost to the shareholders; in Germany employees and creditors come first, while in France there is an even broader remit). A clued-up non-executive director, who has been through these operational minefields, adds a lot of firepower to any merger or hostile bid discussions.

If there is any doubt about this, be sure that shareholders are going to demand and get the right talent advising the chief executive one way or another. And this is especially true in an era of greater transparency, where corporations need to report not only who is on their board, but how much they earn for their input. While this has been a long-standing requirement in the USA, Europe has been able to remain relatively secret. As more cross-border mega-mergers take place and as more non-USA corporations seek a listing on the New York Stock Exchange, so the transparency issue becomes paramount.

Apart from being wise counsel, today's non-executive director brings one, all important attribute to the boardroom – independence of thought. They can think and say things to the CEO that would possibly be "off-limits" to directors who are part of the day-to-day business. This is especially useful where a CEO is a dominant personality. The ability to say, "I think you are wrong about this…" can be very refreshing and very useful. However, it takes a strong CEO to surround him or herself with like-minded tough operators from other businesses. But more and more CEOs are taking this route, as they realize that they need impartial advice from experienced hands – not just the input of consultants.

But getting the right external talent, who can really make a difference in this non-executive role isn't easy – partly because the better they are, the more visible they are and the more people want them. When the head of Pearson, Marjorie Scardino joins the board of America OnLine (AOL) it draws attention. It also shows that AOL want someone in a parallel business to help advise them, especially on their global expansion plans: something Scardino has succeeded in with her own company. When former European commissioner Sir Leon Brittan joins bankers UBS, it just might be because he knows a thing or two about the global marketplace. Often, retiring senior executives are inundated with offers to boost the intellectual capacity and the credibility of a firm by joining the board and meting out advice and contacts six or eight times a year. They can also be useful in turning up great talent by the simple effort of picking up a phone. Most of these people have a rolodex to die for.

However, most of these people are old, seasoned campaigners (recent research in the USA says that the majority of external board members are between 60 and 65), and while they may have a great deal of experience, business today is moving at such a fast pace that their advice can be out-of-date rapidly. Indeed, in fast moving technology companies, in life sciences and entertainment, there is a real need to plug into the thoughts of the new business elite. But, as research shows, most youthful CEOs of start-ups and high technology companies are far too busy to sit on a raft of boards, dispensing pearls of wisdom. Or are they?

What appears to be happening, is that in many cases – particularly in Europe – no-one is actually asking them. Often because they just don't know how to. The main reason for this appears to be that CEOs in the over-50 category (the majority) don't have the links to new businesses or entrepreneurs. Often they themselves are too busy keeping the global business empire together to take a deep interest in boosting the presence on the board of "out-of-the-box" candidates.

But as industry after industry merge into one another (telecommunications, links computers, media and entertainment; retail stores open banks and insurance companies; transportation, lifestyle and leisure firms become one) two things become apparent.

- we all want the same talented people: every industry on earth today wants an e-commerce specialist;
- we all need to look for the next great alliance or merger opportunity; to meld products, processes, people and services.

This means that our boards of directors need external, independent input from the those people who are shaking up our cosy old ways of doing business. We must seek counsel from a broad base of business professionals, young and old, male and female who really and truly can contribute and help us steer a course through the maze of options and opportunities.

Intelligent CEOs who have already "got up and smelled the coffee" (particularly those in the USA) are aware that they cannot always create an intelligent, active board of directors, relevant to the new world business order all by themselves. Increasingly they are turning for assistance to human resource consultants and executive search professionals they know and trust, understanding that:

- they have built up a long-term relationship with the individual, most probably in helping build the top management team;
- they know that these people have a specific talent for finding the people that can be most effective: in this respect recruiting non-executive directors is no different from recruiting a senior employee.

As most CEOs are already aware, we are facing a shortage of effective executives in both the USA and Europe – Asia is no better. Equally, most intelligent CEOs know that they need all the weaponry at their disposal to fight the global business battles of the future. So, if they are intent on building a firm that is rich in intellectual capital, they need a strong board of directors that reflects the future direction and mission of the business. Having a tough, vibrant board of directors enormously enhances the reputation of the firm, boosting recruitment and retention amongst other things.

Remember, no board needs to stay the same forever. There is a strong case in these changing times for bringing in non-executive directors with specific knowledge and experience on short (three to four year) tenures, on the understanding that they will attend a minimum (60%) of board meetings. And don't forget that being a non-executive board member is a two-way deal. While the person will provide a wealth of ideas and commonsense, they, in turn, will learn from this new experience, so it becomes an enriching process for all.

So what are some of the lessons that are being learned about the role of non-executive directors on our boards of management?

- The majority of boards of directors are still bound by tradition. They are virtually all male, all local nationals of the parent and admit few outsiders. Ninety-five percent of all board members in British, French and German companies are local nationals. In the USA that rises to over 99 percent. This is something that needs to change. If you are operating globally, experienced non-executive directors from other regions of the world need to be recruited. The board must cease to be a cosy men's club and become an intellectual powerhouse.

- Firms that were in standalone industries are now in ever more merging markets, where products and services intermix. There is a need to seek out advice from those that can help in understanding the "next big thing."

- New technologies, whole new industries are changing how and why we work. We all need an appreciation of the impact this will have on our business. Don't wait until a CEO retires before you ask him to join the board, catch them young and not necessarily in the top job.

- Finding people to create a dynamic board is going to get tougher. Every organization needs someone responsible for running a proactive nominating committee.

- Boards are not only nationalistic, but sexist too. More and more bright women are making it to the top in some future-critical industries – don't overlook them.

- No-one can keep up with every mover and shaker's climb up the success ladder. The CEO needs someone to do that for them. Consider an inside appointment or a trusted, external professional, who knows your needs and has an extended network of contacts and prospects.

Talent searches, like everything else these days, have gone global. A board with a global perspective that fulfills a role as a strategic adviser, while offering expert and independent opinion, is just as important as having the best marketer, chief financial officer, R&D chief or IT officer. An effective, well functioning board, peopled with relevant skills can be a powerful catalyst, opening the way to new thinking, new opportunities and new markets. And it sends a strong message to future talent, that you are a magnet that others can only envy.

Personal development, another magnet for talent

Every survey in recent years has seen one item at the top of the wish list of why people would join companies – development. Professional, development and personal development are both offerings that will draw talent to your door. Do both of them together, and you are a real winner in the talent magnet stakes. But, let's be careful out there. While survey after survey lists constant training development as a top expectation, we have been in a period where there hasn't been a great deal of talent sitting around without a job.

Development, I feel, is something that employees and prospective employees put at the top of their list when everything else is already there. Once again, it's all about choice. If you know you are highly employable. If you know people want you. If you can command the salary you require and the working conditions as well: then, what comes next? Seems to me it is personal and professional development. Of course, we already know why: "keeping me up-to-date for the day you fire me, because you don't need me any more."

Training and development in the 21st century is, indeed, a strange phenomenon. Back in the 20th century, in the '70s and '80s, if you were in the right job, you got a company car. Now you get sent to Harvard, Wharton, London Business School, INSEAD, or some other executive summer school to show you've arrived.

The bizarre part is with all the job churn currently going on, what company A is doing, is developing Mr High-Flyer for his next job at company B. Because the more your employees get trained, the more of a target they become to other companies. I have no idea how you avoid the vultures gathering, to pick off the tastiest morsels you are serving up! Somehow, it must have been easier when you gave them four wheels to drive and that was the end of your worries.

Having said that, there is no way that any serious organization can hope to miss out on this critical expectation. If you have a well-deserved reputation for giving your people access to the latest thinking and applications in their discipline you are helping boost retention. If you can get others to beat a path to your door (particularly those that are not really looking for a job), because they have heard that you offer exceptional access top development opportunities then you are doing very well indeed. Question is, does anyone monitor this stuff? Do you know what is the real value of having a reputation for personal development in your firm?

Something for the new-age manager

Here's another thought about retaining, but possibly attracting the right kind of talent too.

More and more companies seem to be getting the idea that it might be a smart move to tie part of a manager's bonus to issues like employee turnover.

"You hold onto your people, because they are happy and motivated", goes the argument, "so we reward you."

Great idea. Does it work? Yes, it does.

The concept is simple really. What a firm does is create an employee survey that tracks how they feel, about the business as a whole and what it is doing for them. You then build their satisfaction rating into part – or a whole in some advanced cases – of the bonus or compensation package.

Supporters of the system say that if you don't tie it into something like the manager's compensation, nothing will happen. If you make it clear that the better the result the more bonus the manager gets, you get attention. You get something else too. In fact you get two things:

- Remember all those new-age managers we have identified, that understand what the new-style employee wants from a job? Well they are really good at this stuff, because they really do know how to meet the expectations of their staff. So they are happy, because they get the bonus and then, presumably, they stay longer.

- When the word gets out about how you structure your reward systems, you'll find it a lot easier to hire in more of those type of managers, who understand these new-age employees. They'll have worked out that if you really do reward this way, then you are serious about making it work and that creates all the criteria they need to not only enjoy the job but get paid better too.

Conclusion: pay and compensation aren't simple these days. But, if we want to have our share of talent we are not only going to have to be very flexible and quickly able to tear-up our policies, but realize that, like everything else, companies will be known for what they do and what they don't do. If you do it, tell people about it. If you don't do it, think about what it is costing you by not changing.

Finally, THIS is a GREAT Idea!

When we talk of being, or becoming a magnet for talent, I think that most of us are seeing the big picture. We assume that talent will be drawn to us and then stay with us because of what we are, what we stand for, what are products or services provide to our customers. I think this is wrong.

Over the last couple of years, I have become increasingly aware that many large corporations who should be mega-talent magnets are not. For some reason, the best and brightest seem to shun them, or at least go look and then quickly leave. What's going on?

After talking to many people, I realized that big corporations were – by their own actions – strangling themselves of talent. In their rush to globalize, many, many many multinationals have been doing something else too – standardize.

- Products are the same wherever you go.
- Buying policies are the same.
- Marketing is driven from the center.
- Local-for-local is confined to supervising the translation of the cooking or application instructions.

As a consequence, hot talent is staying away from the big multinationals. Imagine you work in marketing for some major US corporation in their European headquarters in Paris, Brussels or London. What you get each year is a handbook to implement. There is no creativity at all, no chance to do your own thing. Same with products: they are increasingly standardized, built on common platforms. Services too, apart from some legal considerations. A financial vehicle in one market is practically the same in another.

This means that top firms have starved themselves of great people, who have gone into other companies where their contribution has been more appreciated. However, there are signs that the multinationals may have learned their lesson. Led by companies like Coca-Cola they are beginning to realize that the people at headquarters don't know everything, and it is time (again) to let local-for-local campaigns flourish.

This isn't just an issue for the majors. Small and medium-sized companies are having this problem too. Increasingly, smaller companies, especially those that rely on knowledge workers, find that a large part of their day-to-day business is taken up with two, three or four big clients. Again this means that there are many bright, intelligent, eager-to-have-a-go employees who get no real chance to show what they can do. The result? They get frustrated and leave. However, it appears that a solution is at hand. If you really need these people and you don't want to lose them then the solution – already operational in some companies – is to create a series of small projects that will engage these people. Some suggest that even if they are loss leaders they are worth it.

Several organizations I have worked with have done this and found it works. Often it can be a research project that will help them identify future business or begin to develop a product or service that no-one else has time to do. If you need to hold onto talent that you cannot immediately engage consider it.

Same for large multinationals, if you must be global fine. But why not pilot lots of small projects that can be tested in a local market or region and then – if they work – rolled out across the business. Seems like a small price to pay to hold onto talent. Oh, and if the world knows you do that they will beat a path to your door – guaranteed!

7 The top manager's view of talent

The person who knows *how* will always have a job.
The person who knows *why* will always be his boss.

DIANE RAVITCH

First-rate people hire first-rate people.
Second-rate people, hire third-rate people.

LEO ROSTEN

How do bosses run the race for talent?

Ah bosses! Bosses come in all shapes, sizes and temperaments. There are mean bosses and generous bosses, there are bosses who manage by the numbers alone and others who manage through innovation and creation. Every year millions of words are written about the traits of CEOs: what they are like today; what they need to be like in the future.

And what are bosses anyway? Is it the CEO, the leader of the organization, or is it everyone in an organization that has some kind of people responsibility? For the purposes of this discussion about talent, let's for the present concentrate on the *numero uno*, the *capo de capo*, the *grosse legume*, as the French say, and look at how bosses are perceived in leading, or not leading, the race for talent.

In one of those studies that emerges each year with suitable fanfare on both sides of the Atlantic the Economist Intelligence Unit and head-hunters Korn-Ferry predicted that hard-nosed CEOs were headed for extinction. Based on interviews with a couple of hundred companies around the world, their view was that, "more employees must be empowered to self-manage, which can only happen in an environment where goals and desired behaviors are clearly and inspirationally communicated." In plain English that means, "death to the control-freak CEO and hail to the guy that gets us all motivated and excited and allows us to do things on our own." They go on, "Tomorrow's leader will be a team player who will seek to decentralize leadership and work toward creating an entire organization of leaders."

They noted that their research showed that the managers they questioned really believed this was going to take place. In response to the question, "Who will influence your organization ten years from now," they got the following result:

A team of leaders	61%
An unidentified configuration of managers	21%
One leader	14%
Others	4%

Fine, great idea. Has it happened? No.

I think that survey and other research like it showed that the respondents "hoped" it was going to take place. Because the study also admitted that "an overwhelming majority of survey respondents described their present companies' leadership style as command and control." As far as I know, there hasn't been a great deal of sharing at the top. Since that survey was done, many big firms have felt the trembling of the corporate Richter scale. When your stock price goes down the toilet, the team-player spirit is usually flushed away too.

What this and other surveys seem to miss is that we cannot make progress on wishful thinking. Assuming the boss is going to give up being just that – THE BOSS – is naïve. Indeed, a study that I carried out way back in 1979 for *Chief Executive* magazine predicted, over two decades earlier, that we were headed for a softer approach to leadership. Never happened. Oh sure, a few may have tried it, but where are they now, where's their legacy?

Bosses, big bosses, have one thing that most of us mere middle managers don't – a huge ego. In some it is so huge you're actually surprised they can squeeze through doors or climb into the elevator. Sometimes it is hidden or suppressed, but it IS there. And all the evidence points to it. It doesn't matter whether you are in the USA, the UK, France or Germany, most organizations today are run by men (sadly it is almost always men) with ego's that can get quickly bruised.

The urge to merge

The quickest way to get your ego bruised is to come up against someone else intent on showing that their ego, their power, is greater than yours. In recent years and months the financial pages of the newspapers have been littered with these ego battles, especially those linked to take-overs.

Jergen Schemp of Daimler-Benz and Chrysler's Robert Eaton; Jan Leschly of Smith Klein and Glaxo's Richard Sykes; Sandford Weil and John Reed of Citigroup; all have the stamp of big ego bruising battles. In France and Germany it was the bankers beating each other up. Each and every one of them triggered by ego need and an urge to come out of it top dog. What kind of message do these epic, set piece battles send to the troops? What does that do for retention and recruitment? Well, it seems to be both a good and bad thing.

It is a bad thing because if you are on the losing side you usually end up in a period of limbo, not knowing your fate. This is when a lot of really good talent is likely to jump ship. Conversely, it can become a good thing. First, those that are on the winning side are enervated, invigorated and motivated, at least until the first flush of victory has worn off. Second, recruiters will tell you that often unsolicited offers to work come during this time, as many see it as an opportunity to join an aggressive firm that is clearly going places and has a strategy to get there.

So, having a CEO with an ego-drive isn't as bad as some people would suggest. There is another upside. Many managers I have talked to say that if you can face the uncertainty and, yes, an amount of worry it can be a great learning experience. Going through the aftermath of a merger can be a very steep learning curve. The advice is: put on a hard-hat and hunker down out of the way of falling corporate debris. If you come out of the other side intact you will not only have learned a lot but be a very marketable commodity. Companies like people who have been through fire and seen the reality that a merger brings.

It seems natural for people to back a winner. The problems come when you are on the losing side.

The power of the press

Another factor in the talent and the CEO equation is the press. More and more, the media is taking an interest in top managers – mainly CEOs – as legitimate celebrities. Possibly spurred on by the lifestyles, trophy wives and other trappings of success, many of them, notably in the USA are almost as well known as movie and sports stars. But it seems as quickly as some of these modern-day tycoons get built up, the media delights in knocking them down. And this – usually uncalled for – publicity can set all kinds of alarm-bells ringing in employees' heads.

A great case in point is what happened to Luc Vandevelde at troubled British high street retailer Marks and Spencer. With a great track record in Europe, Luc shows up at M&S's London offices to a huge media blitz (he even makes the popular press). Possibly no-one bothered to tell him that M&S has been a British high street icon for more than 30 years. It's troubles in losing market share are keenly followed it would seem by the majority of the British population. As profits begin to slide further, Luc makes more news. He is forced to give back his bonus after media headlines. He is discovered in his very expensive rented apartment in London, and the monthly rental is splashed across the headlines. Luc himself has said he was "totally unprepared for the media coverage" – much of which must have depressed the stock price even further.

What does it do for your business as a talent magnet? Every job hopeful in the land, knows that you have a lousy image, that your product is dull. Does anyone want to work for you? Not if they have the choice. Therefore, companies – and the CEOs – need to understand that you can take a high street icon and through mismanaging the message turn off the tap for talent very, very quickly. For poor old M&S it didn't get any better. Luc then decided to close all their European outlets. Not only did that result in redundant employee outrage and sit-down strikes in stores, but it was roundly condemned in the French parliament. Can you imagine how you would ever recruit again in France if you planned a return some day?

What this shows all too clearly is that CEOs and their communications people need to think through what their actions will do in terms of the image they are about to create. We are ever more transparent as businesses and ever more beholden to the market for our image. We cannot afford to get that wrong.

I can remember the days when no-one wrote about CEOs. They were regarded as grey-faced men who made stuff and weren't interesting at all. But all that has changed. If you are not convinced, think about what happened in Switzerland: venerable names like Swissair, Zurich Financial, Kuoni and Sulzer all coming under scrutiny not just by shareholders but by the media too. In the old days, no-one would have known about it – today it is front page news, even in the popular press. Why? Because more and more people have shares and they are a vocal force. If the CEO manages that in the wrong way he or she has only themselves to blame. If you want to turn away talent, get some bad publicity that everyone has access to.

Consider what happened to Kurt Hellström, CEO of Ericsson, the Swedish multinational. Kurt's business – or the mobile phone business – was spinning out of control. Announcing the axing of 12,000 staff (a larger than expected figure) Kurt was quoted in the world's media as saying, "What we have experienced is the fastest dive in our industry that we have ever seen." He then added, "It's like being hit on the head with something hard."

While we can sympathize with Kurt and his managers, we can only say, OK be honest, but just how honest do you want to be? If you were about to click on the Ericsson website you'd point your mouse elsewhere wouldn't you? You'd save the postage stamp, hold the phone? Talent doesn't want to work for organizations that get "hit on the head with something hard." We want to work with organizations that know where they are going and know how to manage the message to get that through to people.

Remember one thing. When Ericsson's fortunes improve, as I am sure they will eventually, who's going to write long articles about that? For the time being Kurt's the man who got socked in the face with something hard. In the fight for talent, no matter how true that may be, be careful how you say it.

Spin-doctor anyone?

The thought must be that, if our business leaders are going to be part of the talent magnet process, they are going to have to be a lot more aware of the external world than they have been in the past. If politics today is dominated by spin-doctors and making sure that everyone is "on-message", then this new "celebrity status" for our top CEOs is going to need major-management as well.

It is OK to be "surprised" by the media once. It is OK to be "hit on the head by something hard" once. But don't make a habit of it. Not, anyway if you want to be the talent magnet of your industry. And, let's face it, there is nowhere you can hide. Transparency is the order of the day. But, if we need to be transparent, because the analysts, shareholders and media demand it, so we need to look at the other side. We need to make sure that our message, as I argued earlier, is consistent as well as substantive. We need to be sure that it doesn't deviate: we need to make sure we look like winners when we are not.

This is where all those surveys that talk about macho-male leaders being replaced with people with soft (even feminine) skills, and a collection of leaders are so wrong. Talent will flock to a great leader, for whatever reason. Certain people will always want to associate with some kind of success, some kind of vision. No-one is ever going to say, "You know, they've got a really great executive committee, I think I'll see if I can get a job there."

It will never, ever, happen

So what we are going to need to do. Or, to be exact, what the CEO needs to do, is get some talent in to provide that professional expertise. Hopefully free of corporate-word-speak, there is someone that the CEO can trust to stop him or her getting into any problems deeper than they are already.

The two unfortunates I referred to earlier, Luc Vandevelde of M&S and Kurt Hellström of Ericsson don't need that kind of media coverage. What they need is to concentrate on business. If they continue to stumble around the media-shareholder-analyst issue in terms of communication their ability to attract good people is going to be seriously impaired. They need to have a professional on board to focus the firm on where it wants to go and tell the world about that. It can be brutally honest, but still be positive. It can save share price *and* it can stop your best people leaving.

The lessons for CEOs to learn are:

- make sure you know the word on the street, because that is where the talent comes from;

- make sure you learn to manage issues that will get you – very quickly – the wrong reputation;

- corporate life today is too complicated. Get someone to help you (WARNING!! Don't think PR puff-producer!!) on this and – like everything else you do – manage the hell out of it.

Image control

Ultimately, of course, there is only one person sending out the right or wrong signals about the business and that is the CEO. So the more they can be seen around, or the more they are aware of the "beat of the street", the better they can manage the talent issue.

Robert Miller, CEO at giant auto-parts supplier, Federal-Mogul and ex-head of Insurance Company Aetna, says, "if I can have one measure of how a company is doing, it is to go to the store where the company-logo gear is sold. Find out how many people want to wear a Federal-Mogul jacket around their town.

There's another. Go to the bar across from the factory gates and wait for the employees to come out. Ask them what they do. If they love their job's they'll say, "I work for XYZ Corp." If they don't like where they are working they answer, "I'm a product engineer", or the like. The trade, the profession, all too quickly replaces the firm when things start to slide.

CEOs who want to lead from the front and care about talent get their hands dirty and meet the real people. CEOs who want to send out a caring message, don't go to their executive dining room, they mix with the rank-and-file. They find time to lunch with the foot-soldiers in the canteen (often to the fear and trepidation of managers and supervisors) to get a "grass-roots" view of the business. CEOs who do this know only too well that the advantages are huge. They send a message that the CEO cares about what happens. It does wonders for retention, even in the toughest of times.

Stephen Hardis, CEO of Eaton, a 60,000 plus employer of industrial goods and parts, makes sure that his "interventions" into his employees lives doesn't create problems. He says, "I try to organize it the same day. Usually my assistant makes the calls, so that, if they have something already arranged, they can say that, without feeling they have to say 'yes' to me." Robert Miller of Federal-Mogul feels the same, and has closed down the executive dining room. Doing things like this, sends subtle yet, ultimately strong messages to the firm.

Peter Peschak, president Europe of ExxonMobil Chemical, has a wonderful, low-key message-sender hanging on the back of his office door. It's just a hat, but what a hat. Turn up at Peter's office and, more than likely, he'll offer to hang up your jacket or coat. As you leave, you'll notice that on the back of the door is a cap, not unlike a French kepi. Of course, you are prompted to ask, what it is. Peter's reply? "That's the cap I was given when I first went to work for the company in Germany after I graduated. All the employees had to spend time in a service station delivering product to the customer. I have always had it with me, because it reminds me that ultimately, it is the customer who matters most and provides our profits." Now that is a story that underlines a man's belief in his business. A simple story that sends current and would-be talent a powerful message. Not just about the company as a whole, but the individual you work for.

Lessons for every manager

Peter's story is a great lesson for every manager. Yes, you can, personally, make a difference. Your own actions will be perceived by your staff, as well as people on the periphery of your influence. Therefore, it is possible for managers who know how to handle their own part of the business to be little islands of talent magnetism. Even when other parts of the business are suffering adverse comment, you can still hold and hire if you do it right. The main things are to stay consistent and true to the message you develop and make those little things count. You might not hold people forever, but you will be seen as a talent magnet for some, a source of comfort and security to others.

Power poaching

Sadly, corporate life isn't about making people feel good. It is a tough business to be in business these days. And, of course, being seen to be tough is a great magnet too. Tough guys flock to work for people who seem to know what they have to do to make a business a success. If the CEO seems to be on the campaign trail, he or she will take a lot of people along for the ride, because they know if it all works out the rewards will be good.

What CEOs have discovered is that creating a bit of a stir in the marketplace gets the attention of the kind of talent you want to hire. Look at drug company Novartis. They hired an ex Pepsi-Cola marketer Thomas Ebeling as CEO of the company's pharma business, who promptly went out and augmented his team with more than 80 senior hires from the competition. Now that sends a message to the market that you are serious. He then upgraded the medical reps to almost 15,000 worldwide. That sends yet another message. If you want to be in that business Novartis is the place to look.

Different business, similar message to the market. Robert Louis Dreyfus left ad agency Saatchi and Saatchi for sneaker maker Adidas and copycat-ed Ebeling's actions by snatching sneaker-talent from rival Nike. When you do it big-time, you send out big messages that the talent in the industry heeds. So much attention did he get in the marketplace that Adidas is now listed by trend research firm the Intelligence Factory as the number one brand in Europe, another talent driver…. Way to go Robbie!

Money, money, money

Paying yourself a lot of loot as CEO seems to bring little but feelings of envy. Few people seem to think that CEOs deserve all the cash they pay themselves, but it is a phenomenon that looks unlikely to change. The only talent magnet factor in this "super-pay" syndrome is that you might get a few people wanting to join your firm because they think that one day they might make it too.

Years ago, the economist and writer, John Kenneth Galbraith wrote that, "the salary of the chief executive of the large corporation is not a market award for achievement, it is frequently in the nature of a warm personal gesture by the individual to himself." Basically, that still stands true today.

When we see individuals like John Chambers at Cisco, Gerald Levin at AOL, Henry Silverman at Cendant and Jack Welch at GE, pulling down total pay well over $100 million in one year, we should ask ourselves, "are they really worth that amount of money?" Well, they were the ones who negotiated the deals, and so, hopefully, that wasn't the best deal they ever did. However, we also have to ask ourselves what kind of message that sends out to the rest of the workforce. At that level, these people are so removed from day-to-day reality that it is hard to make any kind of judgement. The only question you can reasonably ask yourself is, when are they and the other super-rich top management going to quit? Because the day they do that the talent beacon will take on another color altogether.

Equally, a CEO cashing in on lotsa loot when the business isn't performing, doesn't do any good for being seen as a magnet for talent – a magnet for greed is more likely. Current loser is CEO of Computer Associates, Charles Wang who earned almost $700 million in three years from 1998 to 2000, but produced a shareholder return in that time of minus 68 percent. This does not send good messages.

The real CEO concerns

Having said all that, there is good reason to assume that most CEOs don't spend a great deal of time worrying about the talent issue. At conference after conference it becomes fairly obvious that this is not what is occupying the CEO's brain. But with a war for talent already flaring up, this is seriously frustrating for many human resource and strategic business advisers, who see the inability of CEOs to embrace talent issues as storing up trouble for the future. People in these types of function, like those in the survey I described, are hoping that the CEO will change and spend more time with the soft issues. Problem is, where is the time going to come from?

As many people have said to me, "Get the idea that CEOs who concern themselves with people issues are rare. The others don't care at all, and aren't about to do anything about that anytime soon."

Why is that? Simple. The CEO has too many other things on his or her plate to worry about the people issues. All we can hope to do is persuade the CEO that these issues need attention and get them to sanction a decent budget to get things done. Of course they will pay lip-service to it. Of course they'll sign off the statement in the annual report about the value of people, but they don't spend more than three nano-seconds a day concerning themselves with it. Over the past five years I have interviewed hundreds of CEOs and senior managers in Asia, Europe and the USA. What I have tended to ask them is about their key concerns as CEOs. About what worries them as leaders of thousands of people, when they are lying awake at three in the morning.

Today, I make great play of what CEOs are concerned about when I speak to groups of CEOs. If I were them, I'd have me thrown out. The scary thing is, they don't do that – they laugh. I produced a version of this in an earlier book *Winning the People Wars*, and such was the interest, that I make no apologies of reproducing the list here with an expanded text.

- CONCERN 1 – SHARE PRICE;
- CONCERN 2 – SHARE PRICE;
- CONCERN 3 – SHARE PRICE

We must, as mere mortals, who aren't pulling one or two million a year, realize that share price governs all for the CEO of a publicly traded company. It IS why the CEO exists as the servant of the share price. Yes, share price is the boss of the CEO.

- CONCERN 4 – WHO SHALL WE BUY NEXT?

Share price is up, shareholders happy, analysts happy. We need to make them happier still. Our ego-driven boss decides there is only one thing for it – buy something. It doesn't matter quite what, but we've got to be seen growing not just organically but by acquisition. A good, slick raid and we've sent the analysts home in a good mood again. Of course, we also go out and buy other companies because we are playing copycat games with our competitors. They buy something, we buy something bigger. And so the game goes on.

- CONCERN 5 – WHO'S TRYING TO BUY US?

This is the converse of extreme happiness. Sadly the share price is down and we are in trouble, we are a bargain basement price for any predator circling for an easy killing. CEOs spend a lot of time worrying abut this one and hiring bankers and consultants to consider options for getting out of the mess.

- CONCERN 6 – GETTING READY FOR THE NEXT ANALYST'S MEETING

It doesn't seem to matter whether the share price is up or down, the semi-annual ritual of the analyst's meeting concentrates the mind wonderfully. Once-upon-a-time it was only the CEOs of US corporations who had to worry. No longer. Global business operations mean that analysts have to be wooed by even the most reluctant European and Asian firms. Again, this takes up a great deal of CEO time.

- CONCERN 7 – GETTING READY FOR THE NEXT SHAREHOLDERS MEETING

These can be especially fraught sessions if the analysts have downgraded your stock or something equally evil. As we have seen in recent years shareholders have become much more vociferous in their views and this means that the CEO spends an inordinate amount of time making sure all goes as well as possible. After all, the ultimate folly is to get voted out of the CEO's chair by an angry share-certificate-waving lynch mob.

- CONCERN 8 – INTEGRATING THE COMPANIES YOU JUST BOUGHT

Business has been good and so the CEO went off with his raiding party and bought a bunch of companies that looked good on paper – well, the numbers did. Now the firm is engaged in desperate attempts to integrate just-acquired companies that have very different views of doing business. Thousands and thousands of man hours will go into these efforts.

- CONCERN 9 – KEEPING THE TOP TEAM HAPPY

The CEO has one people issue, the top team. These people need to be massaged and motivated. No CEO can afford the publicity of senior management defections, it sends the wrong message to – you've guessed it – the shareholders and the analysts. The CEO should be worried about the message it sends to the employees.

- CONCERN 10 – WORRYING ABOUT THE RETAINED HOBBY FROM THE DAYS AS MARKETING DIRECTOR

Maybe not all CEOs are ex-marketing, but a lot of them are. Even if they are not, many still seem to succumb to the attractions of external activities. It has always surprised me just how many main board meetings take place on the same dates as golf's Open Championship, the Monaco Grand Prix or Wimbledon. Pick the local airport and go count the corporate jets on the tarmac. It's odd how many hard-nosed CEOs will go gaga at the prospect of dining with Tiger Woods or Michael Schumacher. Maybe it is just the fact that top talent knows no boundaries.

- CONCERN 11 – "WHAT DO YOU MEAN WE KEEP LOSING PEOPLE? GO OUT AND GET SOME MORE!"

This is where the talent issue comes on the CEO's agenda. So all we can really do is pray that he or she has the sense to get some very heavy-hitters in place who can worry about the talent issue on an ongoing basis. Also let's hope that they are given the go-ahead to consider people as a true strategic issue. What is definite is that in the complex business world of today, few CEOs have any time to worry about the concern of people issues. But if it is true that people have replaced capital as the scarce commodity, then they had better make sure that hiring and holding people IS on the top management agenda and that someone with the mind and the muscle to make things happen is put in charge.

Implications for other managers

So how can other managers down the corporate food-chain get people issues in front of the CEO? Answer: not easily. In many companies it seems to take a crisis of some kind. Too often HR managers and the like are scared to tell the truth about attrition rates: or at least they are somewhat economical with the truth.

Recently, I was asked to write a speech for a CEO of a major European firm, who definitely wasn't a people-come-first person. All the same he had been asked to speak to an industry group of his peers about people policies and talent management in his business. While we were talking about what he should say, I asked about attrition rates in his business. I thought it might be useful to use his business as an example, if the percentages looked good. The CEO looked at the HR director who was also with us. The HR director replied, "oh, it's less than three percent." I then asked the CEO if that was true right across the business? He said he didn't know. I suggested it might be useful to find out.

Ten days later, we had our next meeting, to discuss the draft of his speech and, boy was he in a different mood. "You know those attrition figures I gave you?" he said. "Well, they were wrong. Yes, the average IS less than three percent, but we are losing project managers like I've never experienced before, and no-one told me!" He was, rightly, in a real snit. But, it was his own fault. The HR director was protecting his record in retaining people, and no-one else felt comfortable talking about it. What the CEO did was raise the level of the HR job and make certain that attraction and retention issues were on the table every operational board meeting. For that company, project managers were the lifeblood, and they were losing 20 percent a year, because there was a shortage in the marketplace. That's the kind of information top managers need to know, so they mustn't send out the signal that they are going to shoot the messenger.

It is in situations like this that middle managers can find themselves in a quandary, especially where the CEO is hell bent on some major acquisition or other event that takes away from day-to-day business. While it is fine to do the, seemingly, right thing and raise warning signs with as many people as possible it can be difficult to get their attention.

What often has to take place is that managers short circuit the system and just go ahead and "do" things. If they lose key staff, they just have to get new ones. If they need to attract talent into the local market and they get no help, well they just have to do it themselves and damn the consequences. If they do get censored for these type of actions, they have – of course – to ask themselves if they want to remain with the company.

Everything a CEO does sends signals to the organization. Those signals ripple outward to encompass employees friends and family, suppliers, customers and so on. If an organization is fighting to hire the best people, CEOs must decide that they either take on the talent issues themselves or make certain that they have a direct report doing the worrying for them. From now on there will be no way that we can ignore the talent magnet issue. Even at the very top there is no way we can pretend it doesn't exist.

Change at the top

A final point. Managing for being a talent magnet will get tougher not just because there will be less talent to go around. It will also become harder because the tenure of CEOs is going to be shorter. Recent surveys in both the USA and Europe have shown that CEOs don't expect to last as long as their predecessors of a decade ago. Most of them cite shareholder pressure for this development. Indeed, it may well be that we are going to see turnover at the top every three or four years as the norm. What this means is that – except in very rare occasions – there will be frequent changes of corporate policy as new incumbents do it their way. I was reminded of this while writing the book as I was passing Coca-Cola's still-born European headquarters in Brussels. It was commissioned by then CEO Doug Ivester. But enter a new CEO, Doug Daft, who wants everything decentralized and you have a building that Coke's managers will never occupy. Still with Coke, the new CEO is madly keen on local market activity (a u-turn from centralized marketing rules and regulations under his predecessor) and this will send a major message to the market-place. Imagine that you are a young graduate in Madrid, or Munich. Now you have a new place where you can ply your talents, because – unlike last year – they want your ideas. So let's remember that nothing stays very static for long in the world of business. This means that opportunities for talent open and close all the time. What we have to try and do is make these changes as subtle as possible and get the most out of the market without scaring it too much. The changing of the guard of the CEO will play a significant future role in how talent perceives our business.

8 Building tomorrow's talent trap

> There are very few jobs that actually require a penis or a vagina. All other jobs should be open to everybody.
>
> FLORYNCE KENNEDY

> I have sometimes looked with wonder on the jargon of our times wherein those whose minds reside in the past are called "progressive", while those whose minds are vital enough to challenge and to mould the future are dubbed "reactionary."
>
> JOMO KENYATTA

Someone once said, "build a better mousetrap and the world will beat a path to your door." For us in the future there won't be much of a call for mousetraps (how often does your mouse leap out of your hand?), but talent traps are another thing altogether. As I have tried to make clear in the previous chapters, if we don't act right now in turning our business into a talent trap, we are going to have a very hard time of it in the future. If we aren't known today as a great place to work and if we can't begin to put in the systems to keep up that reputation, there is a very real danger that our organizations will shrivel up and die. As plants rely on sunshine and water, so our corporations rely on a ready supply of talent to keep the wheels of innovation turning.

Basically, there are two issues that are going to dominate our businesses in the next decade or so: people and technology.

- People: because they are the new scarce commodity, that's going to get scarcer still.

- Technology: because if we don't use it effectively to make our people better than the competition we will fail.

Add to that, the need to think "flexibility" and "diversity" in everything we do. Whether a CEO, or a newly appointed manager we are going to have to get up each morning ready to think in creative, revolutionary ways. We are going to have to inspire our people to want to come back and work for us tomorrow. So what do we need to do to ensure that talent beats a path to our door? Let's take a look at some of the issues that are going to color our future and make the talent battles of today seem tame.

Everything just got faster

As I outlined earlier, the churn of bodies into and out of corporations is going to increase as everyone either moves on for a more interesting job or gets moved on because their job explodes in their face.

CEOs with log tenure will be rare

Most will either move on because something else comes up that they can do, or increasingly militant shareholders tip them out of the top seat. This will lead to a lot more volatility in the market. Cries of "the king is dead, long live the king!" will be commonplace. And when one king dies, we all know what happens: his closest associates (his top talent) are usually not very far behind. This also means that the new incumbent will often be filling his corridors of power with a whole new set of talent. On top of that, they may well do things a lot differently from the previous top dog, and that means that there will be new opportunities for new types of talent as the organization tries to recreate itself. So, just because you are talented doesn't mean you aren't vulnerable. What is top talent to one CEO is tarnished talent to another. The other phenomenon that will increase in the coming years is the bailing out CEO. Either through boredom ("been there, done that") or having enough loot to do something else, or both. These people pose a threat to the health of many big businesses. Reason? They choose when to bail out and can leave the organization floundering, especially if no successor has been formally named.

Top managers will seek bigger challenges

Other senior managers won't be far behind the CEO in jumping to a new challenge. Increasingly, organizations seeking top talent are prepared to give top echelon operators the work and reward conditions they demand. Signing on for a more challenging job in another city or country rarely means having to uproot your home life for the 21st century high-flyer. Added to that, flexible reward packages that make the most of careful tax planning and stock options are going to be more and more important. It won't be easy for a firm to hold high performers with the kind of offers that will be coming their way. As head-hunters widen their search range, offers are going to come from the most unlikely places.

Middle managers are on the move too

If you want to ring-fence any of your middle management, you'd better do it quick. Whether it is rising stars with great potential or just those super-specialists who keep vital pieces of the business running, they are coming up for grabs, big-time. As the supply-hopper of management potential dries up, rival firms are going to be seeking out your best and brightest further up the age ladder. Forty to 50 year-olds are going to be in the "very vulnerable" category. So you had better run a risk assessment on these people if you want to have any hope of retaining them. Imagine that you are 45 and you are the number two in marketing and – just when you thought that this was as far as you'd get – along comes a great offer. What do you do? You take it. You'll see a lot more of this in the months to come. Flatter a 50 year-old and watch him fly.

Specialists are in a squeeze

There are already strong signs that many specialists are going to be very mobile indeed. Many are falling victim to changes in business strategy and finding themselves surplus to current requirements, so they are already on a career resembling a roller-coaster: well paid one year, struggling the next. Look for this to increase as organizations increasingly learn to use short-term contracts for this type of talent. In parallel, look for the costs to rise as specialist talent exacts higher rates of pay to compensate for downtimes. Similarly, look for a major increase in the use of temporary or "alternative" labor resources. Firms like Addecco and Manpower fully expect this side of their business to grow hugely as employers organize themselves to be as flexible as possible in the specialist talent they need for time-sensitive projects.

Corporate cannon-fodder will survive – just

All things considered the rest of the working world is going to be in turmoil. Corporations are going to be looking for very flexible solutions, so (as above) short-term contracts and other flexi-work offerings will become the norm in many industries. Corporations will defend and lobby for these moves to governments and trade unions by saying (correctly) that employees are demanding more flexible work schedules and they are only meeting this need. However, you are going to have to be smart to make money at this game. Certainly you can have flexi-work but it will come at a price. This again will speed up the pace of the churn of employment as an increasingly large part of the population migrate frequently from one firm to another.

A place to shine

These work trends do, of course, offer wonderful opportunities for employers who can get the work equation for their people just right, i.e. it suits them and it suits the employees too. If you can give just that smidgen more security, a minuscule more flexibility, a better than average development regime and let people know about it, then your star will shine brighter than the rest in the suburban office park. It's going to have to. Everything points to a lot of fights over the scraps of talent we are going to have at our disposal at each and every level.

A dearth of leaders

For a start, we are looking at a talent famine at the top of all our businesses. And what talent we eventually do find to run the company is going to be a lot more occupied than today's CEO in trying to find people who actually want to work there. Two big issues dominate this dearth of leaders, both will demand innovative solutions.

- The 1940's, '50's and '60's baby boomers of Europe, the USA and Japan are quitting their top management positions and heading for retirement communities.

- Fewer and fewer recruits into the business world are prepared to take on people responsibilities.

Is there anything we can do about that?

First, let's consider that instead of making it easy for high-performers to cash in and retire early, we reverse the concept. This was a great idea when you wanted your firm to give off the glow of youth and anything over 45 was ancient. Not now. What our businesses must do – and without delay – is find innovative ways to stem the tide of retirees. Wake up and smell the coffee! You are letting your talent walk out of the door and you are paying them to do it. Even worse, a lot of it is going around the corner and getting some type of deal from your competition to work two days a week from home. Unless your company is in dire, dire straits, please, please, please reverse your early retirement policies now. You cannot afford to lose these people forever. You certainly can't afford to let them take all their knowledge about your business to the competitor you love to hate.

Every CEO needs to urgently review policy on early retirement: in fact policy on retirement period. Don't forget that people don't retire at 65, buy a little cottage in the country and die two years later anymore. Goodness me no. They are still playing golf, jogging and riding around on bicycles at 90. And every year there are more of them, because we all live longer. Believe me, many of them would be happy to have something constructive to do. So get thinking, how can you profit from what they know and what they can still, very usefully, do?

Second, business is going to have to do a major PR job on how great, how fulfilling and how rewarding it is to be a manager; to lead people. The truth is that most wannabe MBAs haven't been told that. What they have been told is that if you want to be successful you stay as far away as you can from anything to do with professional management stuff. Several reasons for that view:

- Managing people is messy. You don't just get to lead them and do the power thing, you sometimes have to fire them and get them to do things that they don't want to do.

- It's a whole lot easier to join a finance house and just be part of a team or be a consultant. Then you can recommend that the dumb managers who are paying you shitloads of money to advise them go fire the people! Hey, that's the way to go, don't you think?

- Most MBA and related programs today concentrate on the number stuff. They turn out the equivalent of very smart accountants, not get-up-and-go managers.

So, CEOs who want leaders are going to have to either put a great deal of collective influence onto the business schools (good luck at that guys!) or they are going to have to promote management as a great career and develop the people themselves. Personally, if I was the CEO, I'd do both – now.

In the past year, I have spoken to a host of worried, disappointed CEOs who regularly visit business schools in Europe and the USA, and their verdict is that they are not going to get too many managers from the classes of 2000, 2001 and 2002. In one case, the CEO asked a classroom of about to graduate MBA students, how many wanted to go into a company as a manager. Not one hand went up! That IS the size of the problem.

On that basis, that there is a huge problem just waiting to happen, here's a few thoughts that might just help. Not only that, it may make you a shining beacon for a new type of talent.

Sell your vision of management in your business

You're going to have to do this anyway as part of the talent magnet so you may as well create it as a key part of the process now. What I am advocating is pretty simple really. If MBA students and the like don't want to get their hands dirty in dealing with people, let's find others who do. And while we are about it, let us use the campaign to do that to send a message about just what a great business we have. Likely as not, you'll not only discover would-be talent that want to be managers, but all kinds of other talent as well.

Will it work? Oh yes. I know, I've done it. Some years ago, a new CEO arrived at a major food company. He was less than pleased with the management he inherited, he found them very set in their ways, unwilling to try new ideas, conservative in the extreme. I was challenged to try and help him access talent.

Here's what we did. The idea is simple and, even better it doesn't cost that much either. In fact, it was done in the days (a decade or so ago) when there wasn't much of a war for talent at all: today, you'd be saving a huge amount in recruiter's fees. What we wanted to do was get this business up high on the image screen of managers across Europe. The new CEO had the idea that if he could create a vision of a great business in the making, talent would find its way to his door.

He was right as it turned out. My job was to create the message and then to create the conditions for the delivery. What happened was that I developed and then honed a presentation that not only talked about the company, but about the management philosophy that made it work. It concluded with the vision and the way forward. I quietly tested the concept and the message on a series of managers to get their reaction. Out of eight people, six said they would love to work for a company like that: two actually asked how they could get an interview.

While this was going on, we negotiated with several conference organizations and a couple of key universities, to get the CEO onto their platforms. Organizations like these love to get CEOs, because they usually have trouble in fitting into their schedules: so we were welcomed with open arms. Then we rigorously rehearsed the CEO, until he knew the presentation backwards. We had five events to present at in a period of four months – February to early June. The total audience at the five events worked out at around 3,000 managers.

Two weeks after the first event, the CEO received 23 letters (this is very pre-e-mail) from managers who said they had been really excited by his presentation, and they were interested in any opportunities to work for the firm. Obviously, he hadn't tried to "sell" the business, but they did know that it was on a fast-track and they also knew where it operated from. By the end of the summer, he had over 200 letters, asking about job opportunities. He hired 42 managers. The cost? Virtually nothing.

All I had done was help him set out his stall and he had done the rest. Not only were they perceived as a magnet for talent, they WERE a magnet for talent. Oh, and there's more. He also achieved a huge amount of press coverage in business magazines and this added to the image we were trying to create of an exciting, innovative business on the edge of being a great place to work.

One word of warning: Don't try and do this if you can't deliver on the promise you make in your presentation. It has to be real or the backlash is huge.

Now, what I am saying for today's world of talent shortages is, don't stop there. Look below those people we were trying to attract in that initiative – and successfully managed to – and get those who might not have really considered a business career at all. Make those speeches and presentations aimed at students in colleges and universities, but make them exciting. Sell, sell, sell. Give them a vision of management as a great, exciting, varied career. There is absolutely no reason why it cannot work just as well as it did all those years ago.

Create your own management development process

Yes, I know most big companies have that already, but I'm not talking about managers you already have. That's training, developing and preaching to the already converted. No, this is different. Go out and find bright, young talent and get it to come to you, rather than let it go and enrol in a business school. All the companies I talk to say that they have big problems recruiting from business schools: the competition is too great, the students don't want to work as managers anyway. Fine, don't play by those rules anymore. Create your own rules and win.

Think about it this way. You can – easily today – build a new *cadre* of managers, by starting your own talent school (you can link it to some accredited school if you like). Why not? What's stopping you? Nothing. Not convinced? Here are a few thoughts:

- there are a lot of top-gun management gurus for hire. What's more with technology, these people can teach in real-time across the globe at the mercy of the web-cam;
- there are literally thousands of leadership programs, courses and course leaders, to help out;
- use your own "best practice" managers as part of the "cast", they know what professional management is all about. On top of that you can make this part of their professional development;
- yes, link up with a business school, but set your own agenda, and get what you want.

The other point to remember, is that we are running out of people anyway. Not just MBA graduates who don't want to be managers, but anyone who wants to go down this route. Therefore, we are going to have to – quite soon – develop very serious plans to take in other options. What this means – and we'll get back to this later in tackling diversity issues – is that there is little point in looking for your "students" in the USA and the EU. You will have to go further – and why not? Eastern Europe (especially the Baltic States of Estonia, Lithuania and Latvia, plus Poland, Hungary and the Czech Republic) is a prime target area. So are parts of Asia. Don't be restricted, do something different.

Is there any reason why you would hesitate? My view is that we will, most certainly, run out of managers in the "west", so we will have to do all this searching for good people in new places very soon anyway. Why not get going now and get a head start? And if you can offer a major commitment to training and development you will be seen as a place to be. My view is that no business that operates outside its national borders can afford not to do this. However, make sure you do tie them down with an agreement to work for your business for at least four years after you develop the hell out of them. Otherwise, it is money down the drain.

But we need leaders ...

Sadly, while all this melt-down of managers is going on, the rank and file are expecting a better performance from those in the driving seat. I doubt this is going to happen, because I doubt there are enough new leaders around to even begin to achieve this. The dean of London Business School, John Quelch, is worried. If he is worried, we should be too. He says that, "the management population is better trained than ever before, particularly in hard analytical skill areas. But, leadership skills are in short supply and this has become a major constraint on the speed with which major multinational companies can expand."

And it is probably a lot worse than that, if only because the few business leaders we have are up against a whole new set of rules that they don't control. I think it's called the New Economy. As Patricia Seemann of Zurich Financial Services points out, "even hard-bitten battle scarred CEOs are rookies in navigating the knowledge era and the New Economy." She adds, "The combination of complexity and limited experience, that virtually all of us (if we are honest) share in abundance, can lead to all sorts of unforced errors and mistakes if we are not careful; or don't understand the ground we are stepping on."

Suggesting that many of our leaders are not really in the driver's seat anymore anyway she points out that, "Understanding the rules and dynamics of the New Economy and deciding how to go out and win it, is not only difficult but can be both intellectually and emotionally wrenching, for both the organization and the individuals who are part of it."

And we wonder why MBAs don't want to be managers?

An anti-business wave

So, don't you think, with these kind of odds stacked against us, that we had better DO something different? Because it is not just a question of running out of people, or running out of people who want to be managers: it is also about a whole group of people who don't want to know anything about business at all.

Every manager – from the very topmost pinnacle to the very, very bottom, needs to consider that, once again, we are getting squeezed for talent. This time it is quite obvious – a lot of people don't want to go into business. They see it as wrong for them, they see it as practically an act of piracy, and they want to do something else instead. We are back to that point where everyone has a choice and increasingly, many would-be young executives are opting for other professional pursuits. Can we win these people back? Doubtful. But, if that is true, then it leaves us with even less of the population pie to carve our futures from. And, you guessed it didn't you, it gets, sort of, worse.

Damn those demographics

Demographics can prove almost anything and often they do. However, there is by now overwhelming evidence that we have not only run out of people but we are going to see a complete famine unless we begin to think about radical solutions.

Here are some numbers to kick-off the thinking process.

- Countries like Spain, Portugal, Italy were exporters of labor, now they import it. In less than one generation they have gone from families that regularly numbered six or seven children to one at most. Childless couples and late-in-life marriages are becoming the norm for the new class of upwardly mobile urban professional. By 2050, Italy could lose practically one-third of its population. In Spain more than 40 percent of the population will be older than 60 by 2050, up from around 20 percent today.

- It's not a phenomenon that's all that new either. Already in 1998, 58 countries reported birth rates below the population replacement level: they included Japan, Russia and China.

- Japan is in a serious population decline. It is now estimated that its population could shrink from 126 million to around 100 million by 2050.

- The European Union's population is expected to drop from 375 million to 330 million by mid-way through the century.

- In contrast, the USA has countered its population decline by allowing more than one million immigrants into the country each year. Forecasts say that by mid-century, its population will rise from 260 million to 350 million.

- To give some idea of the scale of the problem facing the European Union it is estimated by the UN Population Division that it will need a total of more than 13 million immigrants each year until 2050 to maintain the current balance of workers to pensioners. Annual figures for immigrants needed to replace retirees from the workforce in individual EU countries are: France 1.8 m, Germany 3.6 m and the UK 1.2 m.

These figures show clearly why trying to attract talent isn't ever going to be the same again.

Facing up to diversity

The first thing that any manager is going to have to get through his or her head is that we aren't going to be playing by the same set of rules that has served pretty well for the last forty years. That term diversity is going to be much in use.

Strangely enough, few seem to have heard it and even less have done anything about it. As I pointed out earlier, there is absolutely no evidence that any of our westernized companies are doing anything about getting a more diverse spread of people into the business. But, if we want to create any choice at all for ourselves we need to start now.

Let's just remind ourselves that:

- There is no evidence that women are making it into the top talent areas of our businesses in any great numbers.

- Ethnic minorities (especially in Europe) are completely disenfranchised as far as making it into the executive ranks of any mainstream company (the USA is doing better).

- In the public/governmental sector, institutional racism is endemic across the whole of Europe and the USA.

- In virtually every European country the race/immigration issue is the political "hot-potato" that no-one wants to answer. With elections in mainstream EU countries in 2002, there will be battles to both put it on and keep it off the agenda.

The truth is that if we don't allow economic immigration into our countries (the USA seems to have got this message) we are going to be starved of talent. The other side, of course, is that if we do we will starve other nations of the brains they need to develop their own economies. But, it would seem if we are to survive and prosper that we need to open ourselves to a much more diverse workforce. How we do that will be interesting to watch as few businesses seem to have really made much of a start.

I spend a lot of my time at conferences and on company presentations. The audience is usually made up of the senior management groups. While there may be the occasional woman, the rest are usually all white, middle-class male. I realize that I am looking at the last of these "racially cloned" groups. Come the next few years, business will have no choice but to seek a more diverse ethnic mix at both staff, specialist and management level.

This is going to be difficult in many countries for several reasons:

- It will become a *cause célèbre* political issue, which business may want to avoid.
- Tradition-bound management will try and fight it.
- Trade unions will see it as a longer-term threat.

But the talent shortages are not going to go away. Therefore, firms will have only one other choice, if you cannot get them to come to you, you will have no choice but to go to where there is a plentiful supply of top talent, just raring to get to work.

It is not only the ethnic issue that will cause companies to consider what they will do next and, more importantly where they will do it. Labor law will have to be completely revised to meet new needs. If employers are to stay in the USA (where it isn't too bad) and the EU, they must be able to act flexibly. Therefore, lay-off legislation, hiring of foreign workers and work period regulations will have to be more flexible. If they are not, companies will migrate to anywhere they can easily do business. And with a world that is built around instant communication anywhere that is not difficult to achieve.

So where governments are reluctant to bite the bullet and do something about much needed immigration, there will be the ultimate threat of companies leaving and finding other places where they can better organize to be 21st century magnets for talent. When you consider that there will be a shortfall of 1.7 million IT professionals in Europe by 2003, you can begin to sense the size of the problem.

Look at it another way: Germany issued 884 work permits for highly qualified foreign IT specialists in 2000, the industry says it needs 75,000 immediately. Even that paltry number brought protest. Conservative opponents of German chancellor Gerhard Schröder's visa plans have campaigned under the slogan, *Kinder statt Inder* (our children not Indians). Trade unions in Germany are taking the line of demanding increased IT training for Germans rather than importing foreign expertise. Similar blocks to doing anything major to stem the talent shortage are to be seen in France and the UK. And that isn't all. Even if you had an open-door policy, surveys, according to *The Economist*, suggest that many Indian and east European IT professionals are reluctant to emigrate to the EU, and especially to Germany, because of the intolerance and racism they experience there.

There will be others who won't do anything about ethnic diversity anyway, until it is too late. But, be prepared. There is little hope that any company can make it without diversifying not just their labor force, but management levels as well. While many companies are beginning to have diversity programs to increase the numbers of women in middle and senior management roles, few have extended this to include ethnic minorities. Smart CEOs will consider this and do something about it.

Where shortages will bite – HARD!

As I explained earlier, shortages are going to bite western economies hard in areas where given the opportunity, people will move out of poorly paid or unsociable jobs. Teachers, nurses, care workers are all categories where employees are well trained but would be tempted by better work conditions. And that is already happening, leading to shortages in many countries.

The public sector is facing serious recruitment problems, notably because it is a lot less flexible than private enterprise in how quickly it can hire and meet changing expectations about work conditions and rewards.

In the private sector, IT is the obvious area facing major shortfalls of people, but further up the skills chain, marketing specialists, project engineers and general managers are all in increasingly short supply. There is no way that this will change soon.

Has the world seen the future?

Increasingly, I am concerned that these changes are upon us and no-one is really thinking through what will happen next, or what their business needs to do to survive and attract and retain the talent it needs.

The American Management Association, M-World survey, that I have been using throughout, came up with nothing special when asked why companies retain employees. It was, at best, a predictable set of responses.

To the question, "Why do you think companies retain employees?" the respondents said:

They offer high levels of personal development	59%
They offer challenging work	58%
They understand and accommodate employee work/life needs	57%
They offer an exciting work environment	52%
They listen to employee needs and act on them	46%
They are flexible in work policies	40%
They offer above-average salaries and bonus	38%
They offer long-term security	34%
They give extra time off	17%

Is that it? Isn't there more? Shouldn't we have somewhere things like, "The CEO gets what's going on in the world and is getting us ready for it by embracing diversity?" or, "The top management team understand that we need to build a firm as a beacon for talent."

Somehow, somewhere, we have got to start getting worried about all this and we are going to want to work for businesses that seem to know where they want to go and the people they are going to need to get there. Doing it by managing your talent base the way you do today won't work.

Technology and the talent trap

Apart from thinking up new ways to access talent, and finding out how to manage a much more diversified group of people, the other issue that is going to separate the winners from the losers is technology. Managers will have to deploy a far greater array of technology to meet the requirements of being a talent magnet.

It will start with recruitment and finish with tracking former employees. In between, it will help us to create individual employee development programs, allow them to work flexibly and let us interact with a greater number of external suppliers and partnerships.

Let's look at how technology will help us become a magnet for talent in the years to come:

Recruitment

If your firm gets a reputation as a talent magnet, you'll know it. The hits on your website will increase dramatically. But, this never lasts for all that long, sooner or later there are other firms with more magnetism than yours. What we need to do is make sure that current and future technology is working as hard as possible to attract possible new candidates. This means getting involved in website and chat room sponsorship at sites where the types of people you want hang out. A quick look at most corporate websites shows them to be pretty dull fare, which might be fine for getting the attention of a process engineer, but what if you want to get the younger end of the employee scale interested? Another way to do it is through links between your recruitment pages and other sites that job-seekers would naturally go to or to creating your own information sites that link back to "want a job?" pages. Remember, electronic recruitment is cheap. A lot cheaper than using human recruiters – properly developed it can reach out and touch all sorts of people and places you would never have had the opportunity to get to. Other ways of getting people to hit your site are to get books, research and surveys reviewed with a web address. Once interested people get there, you can have a link to current job openings. And, if you can, make it a proactive process. For example, suppose a brand manager hits your site and there are no jobs currently on offer in that category. Make sure that he or she can complete their details, so that if a job comes up you can get them an automatic e-mail that lets them know it's time to apply. Finally, if you have central "jobs open" pages, remember to get the interested enquiries to your subsidiaries quickly. Some kind of electronic dissemination system is vital, otherwise all you create is frustration.

Tracking ex-employees

With the internet, tracking employees is easy. What you need to do is make sure you have their personal e-mail number before they leave and then use that as a conduit to keep in touch. Also having an electronic newsletter for ex-employees can be a useful move. It gives them details of new projects, new contracts, personnel moves and so on, in a quick easy-to-read format. Unless they left under unfortunate circumstances, most ex-employees like to know what's happening. It also makes it a lot easier to get them to consider returning. It is true that many employees who leave find that the grass isn't really all that greener in the next field and they could be looking for a way back but are too proud to do it. This way gives them the opportunity and everyone gets what they want.

Employee development

The reality of the "virtual" corporate university has been with us for some time. But look for this type of initiative to really take-off in the coming years. Time-after-time, employees cite personal development among their top three wants from an employer. If we want to be a talent magnet, we will have to find ways of delivering both personal and professional development to employees scattered around the globe. This has the potential to be a huge differentiator in the bid to be a talent magnet. If you can meet work/life balance needs by allowing employees to work electronically from remote locations and be able to let them access real-time development programs you are fulfilling a large part of their needs. Organizations who can not only do this, but get themselves known as major supporters of this type of initiative are going to win out big. Not only will it be a strong indicator to job-seeking talent, but it will act as a talent retainer too. Additionally, we will be able to create (an already) individual development plan for every employee that they can track via their home PC or laptop. This will show their progress and link it to future opportunities open to them within the business. Assessment and goal setting will become an on-line activity.

Working smarter

Work/life balance issues are set to dominate the wish-list of many employees for the foreseeable future. Technology allows us to meet many of those needs in ways that would have been impossible even five years ago. Ever cheaper telecommunications rates and low-priced hardware and software make working from home, or other remote locations, not only possible but ever easier. Companies that don't have a fixation about "presenteeism" (where they only think the employee is working if they can actually see them) will win out. Results in the future won't be based on how long you work, but the output you've achieved. How you do it, where you do it will be less and less important. Technology will drive that completely, meaning that we will have to embrace new breakthroughs to give our employees the maximum of flexibility and freedom possible.

Working with new partnerships

No company in the future will be able to act alone. Technology will spur us on to being cost-effectively able to link ourselves to other players: suppliers, outsourcers and talented individuals. We will be able to effectively work with people on the other side of the world, building working time that meets the needs of everyone. Managing these new links to the external talent base will become a critical result area for most of our businesses, and hiring and holding the talent to do that will be at the top of many recruiter's lists. Businesses that can do this and are seen to be doing it in a fully committed way, will be the ones that become magnets for talent. Talent that will want to work on the cutting edge of new ways or working and organizing.

We've heard a lot about the "e-thing" in the last few years. It hasn't gone away. It isn't going to go away anytime soon. Whether it is building new links with our employees, suppliers, shareholders or customers, it will be a major enabler of doing business in a more flexible, free fashion.

Expect to spend a lot of time getting the support systems right so that your talent can meet their own and the firm's expectations.

Think the unthinkable – PLEASE!!

In setting out to be a magnet for talent today, we are going to have to begin to think the unthinkable. That, I think, is going to be the hard part. Whether we like it or not, most businesses have a tough time breaking out of the shell they have been hunched in for years. It takes a cataclysm – like imminent bankruptcy – to really force through change of any major, lasting kind.

It doesn't seem to matter if we are partially aware that things are changing around us. We still balk at taking big steps off very high cliffs. While I don't find that at all surprising, I do find it a major concern.

Consider this. In the middle of writing this book I was asked to go to London and meet with a group of senior managers from a broad base of organizations and discuss the issues of recruiting and retaining talent with them. I talked about what companies were doing to hire and hold people. You could see they were skeptical. I could sense their unease. I was an alien in their midst, I was preaching the devil's teachings. Surely it couldn't ever, ever be like that.

Then I realized what was happening. These 50 people (nice, sensible people, I am sure) were in denial. They didn't want to know. I was telling them too much!

When I said, "Can you hire someone you meet on a plane?" they were shocked.

When I suggested that they needed to give their employees the ammunition to work from home, they gasped.

When I said they needed to take an immediate look at diversity (they were all white and male, save for one woman, who was dressed like a man, so didn't count) in the people they employed, they smiled politely.

These people, I discovered (and there are many, many more like them) don't want to believe reality, because they can't deal with reality. They are not ALLOWED to deal with reality.

It happens all the time. I go to a conference of 600 HR managers, and I realize that less than 10 percent of them can do anything about the new realities of business I am telling them about. There may be companies eating their lunch and their mid-morning snack too, but all they can do is stand in the middle of the schoolyard and cry.

Why? Two reasons.

● Reason one is that they can't go back home and tell their boss anything about becoming a talent magnet for the simple reason that the boss doesn't listen to them. They don't have his confidence. If they go in and try and explain this stuff, they will get nowhere.

● Reason two is that they don't have the muscle to push through anything new within the bounds of the job they have. Their hands are tied. To be all modern, let's use that ghastly phrase, "they are not empowered."

Not only are they not empowered, they never will be. They know that it is safer to do nothing, to maintain some long redundant status quo, than to risk life, limb and equity in attempting something new. But then again…

- if it takes nine months to recruit a replacement, you are history;
- if you lose a hot candidate because you are not allowed to go over the pay limits for the job, you are never, ever going to make it;
- if you cannot move quickly to defeat a counter-offer, you are already in division three.

Sad? Of course. But it creates a problem. Because we don't have much choice but to start to do some of these things and we need managers to champion these ideas, to be the organizational revolutionaries.

When I go to conferences or to speak to top management groups, you begin to realize that you are "the entertainment." They have a board meeting, or an "off-site" development weekend and you come along and spend a couple of hours telling them about the weird and wonderful world of work, which, according to them must lie somewhere up the Yellow Brick Road. They don't get it, they don't get the fact that reality is catching up fast with their little fairytale worlds.

While there are a few CEOs who get what's happening and ask me to "please Mike, shake my managers out of their inward-looking complacency" they are few and far between. We have *got* to find ways to get these issues on the strategic agenda.

- We must empower our managers to recruit their own pools of talent.
- We must make it clear that talent attraction and retention are the job of every employee, and we should reward them well for shouldering and delivering on that responsibility.

- We must stop HR managers fiddling with payroll and other administrative "distractions" and help create our business as a place people want to work.

- We must allow our managers to get in the fight for talent and give them the ammunition to do it convincingly. Admitting, "I can't do that, because we are not allowed" is not good enough.

If you haven't already implemented at least some of the actions that are talked about in this book you are in very real trouble. If you want any more evidence, here's why.

Over the next few years, these are the types of things that are going to happen. Maybe not in your enterprise, but they will affect it anyway. They will particularly affect how your business is perceived as a magnet for talent and whether anyone ever bothers to knock on your front door.

We will buy whole teams of talent

Companies in every industrial sector will learn a very quick lesson from the banks and finance houses: why buy one talented individual when you can buy a bunch instead? Possibly spurred on by the fact that banks will start stealing whole teams of product managers and M&A fixers, other industries will get into the action too. You won't just lose your head of budget control, they'll take the whole kit and caboodle. It is even doubtful if you'll have a chance to make a counter-offer. The team leader will conclude the basic deal on a Friday and then over the weekend, propose it to his team. All they need to do is remember the address they need to be at on Monday morning.

Exaggeration? No, possibly understated as a coming threat.

Finally, the talent agent arrives

For years, business magazines have heralded the arrival of the Hollywood-style talent agent on the business scene. Now it is time and you had better sign up your business, before he takes out your talent. Built upon the need of many talented managers to have a career that continues to pose new challenges, these plugged-in individuals will rent-out talent to solve problems and pursue opportunities. Users of the services will be off-limits for poaching talent to fill his stable of super-talent.

Exaggeration? No, it already exists in temporary top manager placements, which will be where it develops from.

… and temporary managers too

Our firms will be built around a close-knit group of talent that organizes and manages a diverse portfolio of preferred people, who are outsourced from temporary agencies. As we develop a new project, we will add talent. When the project is completed, they will go and work elsewhere for their temporary agency.

Exaggeration? No, Firms like Manpower and Addecco already get a large part of their revenues from this type of activity.

A piece of the action

Want to hire great people? Good, then learn to pay them in new ways. Top deal-makers, negotiators and salespeople will demand and get large pieces of the profits of their deals. It will quickly become the norm across all industries.

Exaggeration? No, it already happens in banking, telecommunications, civil engineering, oil exploration, chemicals and transport: let's not talk about military procurement. Just be ready to deal.

Searching the ends of the earth

There will be no limits to where companies will go to find talent to meet their needs. European firms will hire engineers from South America, Asia and Russia; US corporations will plunder South Africa, the Middle East and eastern Europe. A key skill will be integrating diverse cultures into the corporate culture.

Exaggeration? No. One search firm already has an office in Baghdad to search out top-class engineers.

Attacked by an unknown competitor

A competitor we have never heard of (probably from a different industry entirely) will introduce a product or service that will both threaten our market-share and cause a retention crisis with our most vulnerable talent.

Exaggeration? No, it has already happened. Think privatized utilities introducing credit cards, think supermarkets selling petrol, home insurance and giving personal loans.

Your slickest competitor will have the phone, e-mail and snail-mail addresses of all your key employees

Corporate espionage will mushroom to become a niche growth industry, spurred on by the need to replace people quickly and painlessly and get new ideas into a business. Why steal the product formula or the service idea when you can steal the brain that built it?

Exaggeration? No: Already in the USA search firms are diversifying to offer "spying" services that check out the competitor's key employees.

Sharing out your top talent

Letting your top talent work for other firms will be a business-as-usual activity. If you don't do it, you will risk losing them on your team.

Exaggeration? No: It is already happening – in the main with freelance specialists – but has already been seen in cross-over deals in pharmaceuticals, chemicals and transportation.

Get scared, get help

All of these examples are true. All of them are happening right now as you read this book. Also, as you read this book at least one of your key employees is on the phone to a rival company or their recruiting firm. You know it's true, why deny it? We cannot afford to be in denial. If we are, because we know we can't do anything about it where we work, then we should seriously consider going someplace else.

I don't think there is any way to get ready for the talent wars to come if you have your hands tied so you can't stop people leaving and it will take you so long to get more that they will have found a better offer in the meantime.

There's just one thing you might want to consider. Smart companies already have.

The deep, deep down talent audit

It is a fact, that most companies don't know anything about the talent that lies inside their organization. It seems, strangely, that they would rather look on the outside, wasting both time and money, than take the time to see what lies within the perimeter fence of their own business. I mean, when did you last really check-out your own organization? When did you put everyone under the microscope – have you ever?

I think we've already agreed that business has changed and is going to change still further. In fact, the shape and make-up of our businesses is developing all the time. So, it is going to be very much worth your while to find out just what kind of talent you are harboring in your firm: what can it do?; what could it do if it had the opportunity?; how can you organize for that?

A real in-depth talent inventory takes energy and enthusiasm, but it IS worthwhile. Literally it is taking – employee by employee – an inventory of the skills, experiences, expectations and ambitions of ALL your employees. Do it, and you'll be amazed at what you find. Inside virtually every company are rich veins of talent that are underused and underexploited.

As Robert Townsend, author of *Up the Organisation*, the most sensible book ever published about management, said, "most managements complain about the lack of people and go outside to fill key positions. Nonsense! I use the rule of 50 percent. Try to find someone inside the company with a record of success (in any area) and with an appetite for the job. If he looks like 50 percent of what you need, give him the job. In six months he'll have grown the other 50 percent and everyone will be satisfied." Townsend's only error was to use "he." His excuse is that he wrote that comment in the 1960s. An in-depth talent audit today should concentrate as much on "she" as "he."

Think about it this way. What do you need in terms of talent to be successful. Then go looking. Believe me, it is there, right under your nose, only you, and the talent too, don't know it yet.

Once you get a picture of what you've got, there's another step to take: decide which talent you want to tie down above all others. Who are the people you don't want to lose under any circumstances. They don't have to be high-potentials or high-flyers. They may not even have any desire to be promoted or moved from where they are. But they are doing a very critical job in terms of your future plans. Get to know who these people are – at all levels – and have a plan for each and every one of them. A plan that says, "what to do when someone tries to poach Joe or Jane."

Rate them on the vulnerability scale. How likely are they to be stolen, would they go, what would it take (do you think) to keep them where they are? Make sure that you communicate this to other managers. In fact the best idea is to have a management session on this and update it frequently.

The 11C's of Communication

Finally, if you think you are a talent magnet, tell people about it. Make a noise and get people's attention. Sometimes you'll get it wrong. Most times, if you are enthusiastic and show that it's real, you'll get it right.

Communication is too often overlooked – worse still, it is often over-complicated. Honest, open, communication about issues surrounding being a talent magnet are all that it takes. Having spent many years trying to get CEOs and others to take communication seriously (which by and large they don't) I have come to the conclusion that there are eleven points to effective communication inside a business. Neatly enough they all happen to begin with "C" (now isn't that a coincidence!).

- Clear
- Concise
- Consistent
- Constant
- Candid
- Conspicuous
- Credible
- Categorized
- Current
- Cheerful
- Chatty

Do these well and with enthusiasm and you could even be forgiven for a lack of professionalism! By that I mean, that in so many cases there isn't a professional communicator (whatever that may be!) around. There's no PR agency or person from the communications department to help. You, Mr and Ms Manager are on your own. How do you get that message across; how do you get the idea to people that "hey, we are working in a pretty good place, let's stay a while."?

Clear

Start from the idea, "what do I want people to understand?" "what should they take away from this communication?" Too many employee communications are too long, too complex and too, too boring. If you are not a professional (and there aren't any available), write it in a narrative form. Think: "how would I say it to people?"

Keep it *clear*.

Concise

For goodness sake keep it short. Most people's attention spans are tiny. If you want to get the message across, get their attention and then get out.

Keep it *clear*, keep it *short*.

Consistent

Remember what you said before. Maintain a link between the last communication and the next. Above all, don't get caught out with new messages wrapped up in "sugar-candy" pills. It doesn't work and it insults the intelligence of people.

Keep it *clear*, keep it *short*, keep it *the same*.

Constant

Don't stop – ever. Keep the news in front of people. Keep your hopes and dreams, successes and failures right up there. People don't respond to occasional communication, it makes for suspicion. "They only tell us something when they want something," is a view I hear a lot. Smart communicators lay it on the line, all the time. Not too much, but whenever there's a good reason. And most times there is.

Keep it *clear*, keep it *short*, keep it *the same*, keep it *going*.

Candid

Above all be honest. If you don't tell the truth your employees – plus the rest of the world – will find you out. We live in a world where any attempt to hide information is useless. Not only are the best employees well-informed and intelligent, but most of the rest are too … Don't insult people, tell the truth, and tell it when in happens. Above all don't try and influence, or massage the message – employees will see through you.

Keep it *clear*, keep it *short*, keep it *the same*, keep it *going*, keep it *honest*.

Conspicuous

Make sure that what you want to tell them gets seen and gets read. Don't try and be subtle. People get too many messages each day to want to read only yours. Your job is to get that communication in front of your employees and understood, any way you can.

Keep it *clear*, keep it *short*, keep it *the same*, keep it *going*, keep it *honest*, keep it *visible*.

Credible

In addition to being honest, be credible. Employees know that if it's too good to be true it probably is! Top managers need to understand (PLEASE!) that messages that are simple, and straightforward tend to work. Long messages DON'T.

Keep it *clear*, keep it *short*, keep it *the same*, keep it *going*, keep it *honest*, keep it *visible*, keep it *credible*.

Categorized

Don't try and sell the same story to everyone – it doesn't work. Sell the same message, not the same way to tell the story. Give the people at different levels the story that they want to read, that they can absorb, that means something to them, that is acceptable to them. Categorize your message to the groups that you need to explain the story to.

Keep it *clear*, keep it *short*, keep it *the same*, keep it *going*, keep it *honest*, keep it *visible*, keep it *credible*, and keep it *categorized*.

Current

Never, ever wait to tell the story. These days immediate action is called for. Tip: if for all sorts of reasons you can't tell everything, tell something. If there is a communications vacuum it always gets filled with gossip and speculation. Why? Because rumors are always more interesting than the truth.

Keep it *clear*, keep it *short*, keep it *the same*, keep it *going*, keep it *honest*, keep it *visible*, keep it *credible*, keep it *categorized*, keep it *current*.

Cheerful

Not a good word, cheerful, but it works for this stuff. Stay positive, keep it as light as possible, don't turn your message into some Wagnerian opus. Just keep it COOL. Don't listen to the doomsayers and the control freaks, keep it on message but with the slant firmly focussed on the upside.

Keep it *clear*, keep it *short*, keep it *the same*, keep it *going*, keep it *honest*, keep it *visible*, keep it *credible*, keep it *categorized*, keep it *current*, and keep it *cheerful*.

Chatty

When in doubt how to say something, just write it like you would speak it. Just use your own words. Many of us don't have access to communications professionals in our day-to-day work, so think about what would make sense to you … Think of the messages that you respond to.

Keep it *clear*, keep it *short*, keep it *the same*, keep it *going*, keep it *honest*, keep it *visible*, keep it *credible*, keep it *categorized*, keep it *current*, keep it *cheerful*, and keep it *chatty*.

Conclusion

There is no doubt in my mind that we are going to have to spend a lot more time of finding ways to be a talent magnet. More than that, we are going to have to discover new ways to make people want to stay with us – even when we are not doing the best business in the world. But, it is better to tell your troops that you are hurting, than to wait until they find out about it. Believe me a pissed-off, but fully informed employee, is a lot better than a pissed-off, totally ignorant employee.

Here's an idea to try as the battle for talent gets worse. Create a compelling vision of tomorrow, even when you are under heavy enemy fire. By that, I mean, tell them what it is going to be like when you have won the latest battle. Give them a view of "what the dawn will look like when we have been through the night."

If you've done all the right things to hire and hold your talent. If you are a true talent magnet, people won't just drift off at the first sign of trouble. They'll dig in and stay. Hey "they'll even relish the experience." Just try and make it easy for them to stay.

Remember, you don't have 100, 1,000, 10,000 or 100,000 employees, you have individuals. All of them have their own needs and expectations and they want them addressed – individually and with understanding. Do that and they'll be the best advertisement for your business you have ever seen.

Index